Girl Talk

Girl Talk

Getting Past
the Chitchat

A Modern Girl's Bible Study
Refreshingly Unique

JEN HATMAKER

NAVPRESS®

BRINGING TRUTH TO LIFE

The Navigators is an international Christian organization. Our mission is to advance the gospel of Jesus and His kingdom into the nations through spiritual generations of laborers living and discipling among the lost. We see a vital movement of the gospel, fueled by prevailing prayer, flowing freely through relational networks and out into the nations where workers for the kingdom are next door to everywhere.

NavPress is the publishing ministry of The Navigators. The mission of NavPress is to reach, disciple, and equip people to know Christ and make Him known by publishing life-related materials that are biblically rooted and culturally relevant. Our vision is to stimulate spiritual transformation through every product we publish.

© 2007 by Jennifer Hatmaker

All rights reserved. No part of this publication may be reproduced in any form without written permission from NavPress, P.O. Box 35001, Colorado Springs, CO 80935. www.navpress.com

NAVPRESS, BRINGING TRUTH TO LIFE, and the NAVPRESS logo are registered trademarks of NavPress. Absence of ® in connection with marks of NavPress or other parties does not indicate an absence of registration of those marks.

ISBN-13: 978-1-57683-895-2
ISBN-10: 1-57683-895-1

Cover design by The DesignWorks Group, Wes Youssi, www.thedesignworksgroup.com
Cover image by Shutterstock
Creative Team: Terry Behimer, Karen Lee-Thorp, Kathy Mosier, Darla Hightower, Arvid Wallen, Kathy Guist

Some of the anecdotal illustrations in this book are true to life and are included with the permission of the persons involved. All other illustrations are composites of real situations, and any resemblance to people living or dead is coincidental.

Unless otherwise identified, all Scripture quotations in this publication are taken from the HOLY BIBLE: NEW INTERNATIONAL VERSION® (NIV®). Copyright © 1973, 1978, 1984 by International Bible Society. Used by permission of Zondervan Publishing House. All rights reserved. Other versions used include: the *New American Standard Bible* (NASB), © The Lockman Foundation 1960, 1962, 1963, 1968, 1971, 1972, 1973, 1975, 1977, 1995; the *Contemporary English Version* (CEV) © 1995 by American Bible Society. Used by permission; *THE MESSAGE* (MSG). Copyright © 1993, 1994, 1995, 1996, 2000, 2001, 2002, 2005. Used by permission of NavPress Publishing Group; the *New Life Version* (NLV) copyright © 1969 by Christian Literature International; and the *Holy Bible*, New Living Translation (NLT), copyright © 1996. Used by permission of Tyndale House Publishers, Inc., Wheaton, Illinois 60189. All rights reserved. All italics are the author's. The study is best followed using an NIV Bible.

Printed in the United States of America

1 2 3 4 5 6 7 8 / 11 10 09 08 07

FOR A FREE CATALOG OF NAVPRESS BOOKS & BIBLE STUDIES, CALL
1-800-366-7788 (USA) OR 1-800-839-4769 (CANADA).

For my girlfriends and the ties that bind us—chips and queso, motherhood, God's Word, laughter, honesty, a smorgasbord of vices, ministry, road trips, prayer, transparency, silliness, happiness, and togetherness. You speak blessings into my life worthy of heaven. I love you. I treasure you. I thank you.

Contents

WEEK THREE: WHERE HAVE ALL THE GOOD PEOPLE GONE?

WEEK FOUR: THE GIFT OF GAB

WEEK FIVE: FRIENDSHIP BUILDERS

Acknowledgments

I want to thank my mom and grandma for teaching me the value of girlfriends. Your friends have changed my diapers, raised me, taken me to the ER, cheered at my games, taken vacations with us, cried at my graduations, cried at my wedding, held my babies, and sent me into ministry like I was their own daughter. Thank you for traveling through life with your own girlfriends. I learned well from you both.

Thank you, Brandon, for giving me the gift of time with friends. It doesn't matter that you buy Oreos and Pringles the second I leave; I don't care if the kids take baths or brush their teeth. For the space to be with my girlfriends, thank you. You can't imagine how many conversations they've taken off your plate. I love you.

I'm grateful to my sisters, Lindsay and Cortney. Although fifteen years ago I swore I'd never forgive you for ruining all my clothes and embarrassing me in front of my friends, guess what? We're friends now. It really happened. We're so mature and grown-up. I love you.

Thank you to my best people at NavPress: my editor, Karen Lee-Thorp, who is swift and calculating with that insert

9

comment key, Terry Behimer (I'll miss you), Kris Wallen, Pamela Mendoza, Kathy Mosier, Kristen Baldini, Kate Epperson, Arvid Wallen, Eric Grogg, and every other wonderful person who turned this typing into a book and saw that it got to a shelf. You are talented, supportive, fantastic, encouraging. I'd love to give you a fat bonus, but as you know, Christian writers don't make any money.

Finally, I want to thank God for coming up with the idea of girlfriends. Salvation, forgiveness, grace, eternity . . . oh, no! That wasn't enough. You gave us the gift of unity, and I, for one, love You so much for that. For forming us to laugh and love, I am utterly grateful. You're the best Creator ever.

Introduction

Welcome, Modern Girls! This might be one of my favorite projects ever. I once thought of the pursuit of holiness as a hodgepodge of repentance, humility, and discipline wrapped tightly in Sunday school attendance, Christian conferences, and three hours of Bible study each day. If I snuck in some fun, well, I'd confess it later.

So it's been amazing to discover that friendship among women is an avenue to godliness, too. It's not a luxury I should feel guilty about prioritizing. It's not frivolous when we tell funny stories until one friend snorts Diet Coke out of her nose. It's not a waste of time to sit with a friend and have no agenda other than knowing her. In fact, friendship mimics the very intimacy between the Father and the Son.

I had a conversation earlier this year that cemented this subject as my next Bible study. A woman I consider hilarious, approachable, and authentic in every way shared her fear of friendship with me through tears and raw fear. Barely able to get the words out, she kept repeating, "I can't." She honestly disclosed the veiled approaches she took with friends. But by the next day, the tears were cleaned up and everything was "fine."

My heart broke wide open.

I have yet to get that conversation out of my head.

Oh, Dear Girlfriends, let me help you discover the laugh-out-loud joys of real friendship. Are there some scary parts? Sure. A few. But there are so many wonderful parts that the risk isn't worth losing one day over. Not one solitary day. I don't want to think about taking a single breath without my girlfriends. They fill a place in me that is theirs alone to fill. If I don't let them in, that place will remain empty.

Travel with me during the next five weeks as we cast off what holds us back and put on what leads us forward together. Unity is not just a good idea; it's not a bonus addition once you have the time or inclination. It is the design and desire of God. Paul expressed this in his letter to the Philippians: "Make my joy complete by being like-minded, having the same love, being one in spirit and purpose" (2:2).

You'll encounter three icons throughout the study representing three different ways to respond. The radio icon indicates a time to dig into the Word, the rearview mirror icon offers a chance to personally reflect on truth, and the telephone icon opens the door to intimate prayer. The questions with asterisks throughout the study are good discussion starters if you'll be meeting with a small group. In addition to the book you're holding, you'll need a Bible and a lined journal for your answers and journaling activities.

Walk with me, Girlfriend.

WEEK ONE

Together

The Friend in Every Girl

A couple of summers ago it became clear that my days of flimsy twenty-dollar swimsuits were over. They kept my boobs hovering around my navel, and my butt was falling out the back side. Three children and gravity had taken their toll, and I simply needed more containment. So rather than shopping at Target (God's store), I went to a high-end boutique to see what the other half wore to the lake.

Soon enough, I found it. It was firm. It was tight. It was basically made of trampoline material. Body parts were within a few inches of their rightful place. It was glorious. Until I looked at the price tag: $130.

Oh.

My.

Stars.

Well, I simply wouldn't spend that much on spandex. No. No. I wouldn't. I couldn't. I wasn't that ridiculous. People were starving in Africa, and, plus, I didn't want my husband to divorce me. I walked around with it, fretting for ten minutes, made peace with my destiny as a single mom, and bought it.

I wasn't four steps away from the register when I yanked out my cell phone because as any girl knows, this was a crisis, and it required a girlfriend. I called my Girlfriend Trina:

Trina: Hello?
Jen: I just spent $130 on a swimsuit. Is there any way you can make this okay for me?
Trina *(without even hesitating or gasping)*: It props your boobs up. It makes your stomach look flat. It holds your butt in. It conceals your flab. It's cheaper than a gym membership. Price per wear is like six cents. Plastic surgery would be too vain — you obviously have no choice. Heidi Klum bought a swimsuit for $900, so yours is practically free. You cannot put a price on confidence.
Jen: I love you.
Trina: I know.

So while my husband was lying on the floor having a coronary that night, I told him, "Trina says you can't put a price on confidence." It was little consolation.

In all the world, there is hardly anything more valuable, more dear, more treasured than friendship among women. It is the glue that has held us together since the beginning of time. Women will sacrifice, risk, stand on the ledge for the sake of real relationship.

While men value self-sufficiency, women literally define themselves by their relationships: I am a mom of three, a wife of twelve years, the oldest daughter, a sister to three, a girlfriend. Or: My son and I are at odds. I'm alone right now. I'm dating someone. My friends seem too busy for me. My husband and I are struggling.

This is who we are.

In *Captivating*, John and Stasi Eldredge wrote, "This is so second nature, so assumed among women, that it goes unnoticed by them. They care more about relationships than just about anything else."[1]

*On a scale from 1 to 10 (1 is utterly detached; 10 is completely knit together with others), how relational are you?

How does the quality of your relationships affect your life?

I'd love to see your answers, Girlfriends, because I know they run the gamut from "I don't need people" to "I need people like I need oxygen." I also know those answers weren't derived in a vacuum. Many factors affect our relationships: our parents, our childhoods, our history with other women, our experiences with betrayal and abandonment, our modern feminine quest for independence. The fabric of friendship becomes complex with each new layer.

But it's easy to boil friendship down to its pure form; just watch two little girls. Free from baggage, fear, the tendency to pretend and posture, little girls are unhindered in their natural desire for friendship. My six-year-old, Sydney, ran out from the McDonald's playground flushed with happiness and declared, "Mommy! I made a new best friend! We *love* each other!" She pointed to a little girl with a head of black braids who was waving through the window.

"How nice, honey! What's her name?"

"I don't know."

It's just that simple. There are no complicated issues to work through, no walls to guard. Let's hold hands and skip. Let's tell our secrets. Let's play and enjoy each other. While little boys play war and adventure, little girls sit knee to knee and giggle.

Jesus explored this same line of thinking, Girls. A concept is often best taught through the pure, uncontaminated experience of a child.

 Read Matthew 18:1 and the background info in Mark 9:33-34. What emotions or insecurities prompted the disciples to ask this question?

How do these same hang-ups hinder authentic friendships now?

Selfishness is our natural drift. The first woman to walk this planet had the same urge for self-preservation and self-advancement. If we don't look out for number one, others will take advantage of us. We'll get left behind. Stepped on. Passed over. Used up. Left too vulnerable. Hurt. But if we can be the greatest in our relationships, there is no risk.

Being the greatest in friendship takes on several forms. Sometimes it means showing no weakness, always being the listener, the counselor, the fixer. Or maybe it manifests itself as fierce independence: "I don't really need you." Often it shows up as we ramrod our own interests down our friends' throats. Differences threaten the insecure. Usually it masquerades behind a glossy facade: "Everything is fine. Life is wonderful. It's great to be me."

Being the greatest has some traveling companions: jealousy, insecurity, bitterness, pride, bare-naked fear. These keep us posturing and pretending, and they lock us down in isolation. This is certainly true of friendship, but it's also true of every relationship where the first concern is how high up a person can stay.

 Is this a struggle for you? In what ways does it show up in your relationships?

Read Matthew 18:2-5. What was Jesus saying about being the greatest?

How do those truths transfer to friendships?

Mark tells us that the disciples argued about this issue as they walked behind Jesus on their way to Capernaum. Jesus' keen ears hadn't missed it. So He had plenty of time to think about how to lead them. How would He teach? What would be the most profound message? Out of all the possible comparisons He could use, Jesus chose a child's experience.

I bet the disciples were fuming. There they were, trying to get up higher, and Jesus told them to be like a little boy. Unassuming, unpretentious, open, honest—these don't pave the way for greatness as we see it. And we can't be trusting and truthful with careers, circumstances, possessions. No, we express these qualities only in relationships, the very place we fear them most.

*List every advantage you see to approaching friendship as a little girl would. Try to uncover what Jesus was getting at.

List the disadvantages to this approach as you see it.

Those disadvantages keep us paralyzed, don't they? In my Thursday night Bible study, we were discussing the ugliest areas of our hearts. It was raw and unfiltered. My Girlfriend Carson had that frozen look on her face, and she finally said, "I'm trying to decide whether to tell the truth or make something up." We all laughed, but we all understood. Being the greatest constantly conflicts with truth. It keeps everything a little shinier, but at the end of the day, the real you never shows up.

Maturity requires parts of us to remain childlike while other parts grow in wisdom and discernment. Don't mistake Jesus' counsel for naïveté; He never asked us to be foolish. When Jesus first sent His disciples out to minister, He told them, "I am sending you out like sheep among wolves. Therefore be as shrewd as snakes and as innocent as doves" (Matthew 10:16). These two traits *can* coexist.

In friendship, do you tend toward optimism or skepticism? Either way, how has it affected the quality of your friendships?

That balance is our goal for this study, Girlfriends. We will reclaim the purity of friendship among little girls, while training our hearts to discern safe relationships. And though parts of our study will involve practical steps, my aim is to uncover that place in friendship that seems magical, even mystical. That place where God knits the hearts of women together in such a spiritual way that we take part in the holiness of relationship, not unlike the bond between Father and Son.

Whatever your history with other women, I welcome you here, Friend. I ask only that the real you show up. Bring your hurts, your joys, your fears to this moment in your journey. Remember, Jesus told His disciples, "Unless you *change* and become like little children . . ." (Matthew 18:3). He knew that to possess the mysteries of heaven, we'd have to transform. There is no other way.

The good news is that spiritual change is rooted in the blessed power of the Holy Spirit, the very power that turns us into God's daughters. You are not alone on this divine path of relationship. The Spirit beckons you; He'll hold your hand as you cautiously step forward. And He'll walk with you until you can reach out and journey on with your girlfriends.

Thank God for bringing you to this study, however you got here. Pray for truth to win you over as you travel on. Ask the Spirit to help you move forward from the place where you currently are.

God's Game Plan

*I*t's weird that God called me to writing, because it requires so much isolation. Some writers are reclusive by nature; they hole up in their cabins drinking gallons of vodka and refusing hygiene and human contact. But I am the exact opposite, save the vodka. (That was a joke.)

When my last deadline was approaching, I'd worked around the clock for days. I hadn't taken a single phone call or left the house. Near the end, my husband deposited our three kids at my Girlfriend Trina's house so I could work without distractions. After a few hours, I called Trina and asked if I could come over. Brandon looked at me like the mental patient I resembled and said, "Why do you want to go there? All our kids are there! It's quiet *here*!" With a melodramatic lump in my throat, I cried, "I'm sick of myself! I'm sick of silence! I just need a girlfriend!"

At Creation, God declared everything He made good — the light, seas, plants, stars, animals, and finally the man He fashioned. It was all good. Adam began working in the Garden of Eden, walking along the river, tending the land. From God's own mouth, creation was declared good, good, good.

Until God watched Adam begin the business of living. No, this wouldn't do. There was a void, a piece of perfection not yet designed. Adam's productivity was impressive; his physical abilities weren't lacking. The animals were getting along fine. The natural order God established was flawless. The cycles were balanced. The vegetation was flourishing. The sounds, the smells—earth was a masterpiece. It looked like paradise, yet . . .

God declared, "It is not good for the man to be alone." Creation was incomplete until humanity was placed together. With Eve, it was truly good. Oh, Girls, it is not good for people to be alone. Isolation is not good. Loneliness is not good. Self-absorption is not good. The last time a human was alone with God's blessing, there was only one man on the planet. Since the creation of Eve, God has set us in community.

Read Ephesians 4:1-3. How would you define "unity of the Spirit"? What is that?

A few synonyms for *unity* are *agreement, unison, unanimity, conformity*. Unison? Christians are about the most diverse group on the planet. I suppose that's why Paul used words like "completely humble," "gentle," and "patient." Peace is the bonding agent among believers, no matter their differences. Peace can exist between conservatives and liberals, Baptists and Catholics, Americans and Europeans, old schoolers and new schoolers.

It can because the Spirit is able.

Henri Nouwen wrote,

Community is first and foremost a gift of the Holy Spirit, not built upon mutual compatibility, shared affection or common interests, but upon having received the same divine breath, having been given a heart set aflame by the same divine fire and having been embraced by the same divine love. It is the God-within who brings us into communion with each other and makes us one. It consoles us with the revelation that God indeed does want to create among us the unity we most long for.[2]

If the Spirit is powerful 'enough to wash a filthy sinner pure as snow and present her to the Father as a specimen of holiness, *worthy of eternity*, then He can bridge the gap between a hymn lover and an electric guitarist. Do our style preferences matter? Does my denomination require a wall of separation? Does the color of our skin make any difference in God's holy nation? Where you live, how I worship, where they minister—how have these so fractured the family of God? As Paul reminded us, "For this reason I kneel before the Father, from whom his whole family in heaven and on earth derives its name" (Ephesians 3:14-15).

*On a broad scale, how have you dealt with differences in the whole family of God? Judgmentally? Patiently? Critically? Humbly? Why have you responded this way?

Read Ephesians 4:4-6. Continuing Paul's theme, list everything you can think of that is the same among all believers. How are we truly one?

Believer, we are one in all the ways that matter. It's time to get off our self-righteous soapboxes and live a life worthy of this sacred unity. God has set us in a community of the rescued. What we have in common is enough to celebrate for eternity, yet we prefer to focus on our differences, spewing pride and dissention. And we wonder why the rest of the world doesn't want to be around Christians.

Girls, the family of God was designed for joy and together-ness on a grand scale. We are to draw together as we draw near to Jesus. I dare you to read two pages of the New Testament and not acknowledge the holiness of community. The entire Word screams this truth.

Godliness is not an individual journey. If it were, then who is all that love for? What is all that service about? Who are we to be patient, gentle, and honest with? Who are we to be kind, compassionate, forgiving, and joyful toward? Why do we have to get rid of bitterness and rage? Why do we need to learn about sacrifice? Who are our spiritual gifts for?

What is the point of community?

Read Ephesians 4:7,11-13. Paul moves from "one" to "each one" now. List every reason for community you see here.

My teachers have prepared me for works of service—they've given me passion for God's Word and the tools to unpack it. Some taught me from the pulpit; others taught me over coffee. My girlfriends have exercised grace to me in hundreds of ways. In my community of faith, I've been built up. I've been loved. My knowledge of Jesus has stretched infinitely. Without God's family surrounding me, raising me, challenging me, I would've settled for my own limited perspective on God's Word, alone in my ugly behavior and terribly lonely.

Harry Stack Sullivan, an eminent psychiatrist, proposes that all personal growth, damage and regression, and healing come through our relationships with others. By ourselves, we can only be consumed by selfishness and suffer shipwreck. Who we are at any given moment will be determined by our relationships with those who love us or refuse to love us and with those we love or refuse to love.[3]

*Do you experience the benefits of Christian community Paul described? If so, how have they affected you? If not, what has kept you from them?

I've never met anyone who detached himself or herself from God's church and became better for it. Though it's trendy to separate Jesus from His church and claim a purer faith, worship void of human error, "All I need is Jesus" is a load of bull. Jesus said the same thing: "I pray also for those who will believe in me through their message, that all of them may be one, Father, just as you are in me and I am in you. . . . May they be brought to complete unity to let the world know that you sent me and have loved them even as you have loved me" (John 17:20-21,23). To forsake Jesus' church—the one He died for—is to forsake Jesus.

It is not possible to be a growing believer without joining your heart with other Christians. If you think you are, you are being deceived, Friend. God's heartbeat is for community. Every single command in the Bible was summed up in two life views: (1) love God and (2) love others. It's not a gray area.

It is through believers' love for each other that God teaches the world. We are living demonstrations of compassion, forgiveness, selflessness—lessons this world is in dire need of. Community is where Jesus strengthens us through His other disciples. It's the village that raises our children together in God's family. It's where the lost, broken, orphaned, and left behind can find open arms. "God sets the lonely in families" (Psalm 68:6).

We are that family.

Ask God to show you how He feels about community. Ask Him to help you release any misconceptions or bitterness you have toward His family.

Satan's Game Plan

Noam Chomsky, a linguistics professor at MIT and a well-known political activist, discussed the war strategy of divide and conquer:

> Naturally, any conqueror is going to play one group against another. . . . Just take a look at the Nazi conquest of nice, civilized Western Europe. . . . Who was rounding up the Jews? Local people, often. In France they were rounding them up faster than the Nazis could handle them. The Nazis also used Jews to control Jews. . . .
>
> That's the traditional pattern. Invaders quite typically use collaborators to run things for them. They very naturally play upon any existing rivalries and hostilities to get one group to work for them against others. . . .
>
> These are people who are being crushed and destroyed from every direction. If they grasp at some straw for survival, it's not surprising—even if grasping

at that straw means helping to kill people like their cousins across the border.

That's the way conquerors work. They've always worked that way.[4]

Chomsky is certainly no theologian, but he described Satan's attack on the Christian community as well as I've ever heard it, even if being quoted in a Bible study gives him an aneurism. Sweet Girls, we are under severe attack, whether you're aware of it or not. If you understand God's desire for community, you can imagine the Enemy will have a war strategy for ruining it. And he does.

Divide and conquer.

How do you see this strategy at work in God's family, maybe even in your church?

The church at Corinth was founded by Paul, but it quickly wrestled with immorality and disunity. Corinth was Sin City, and new believers floundered on how to deal with each other, with sin, with life as Christians. What's new?

Now someone in their church had caused serious pain. We don't know who or what, but Paul heard about it after he left them. Maybe the offender verbally attacked another believer. Perhaps he stirred up dissention within their young church. Maybe he lied maliciously or spread rumors. We don't know, but the church confronted him as Paul instructed, and he was fragmented from the other believers. After this heartache, Paul wrote 2 Corinthians.

Read 2 Corinthians 2:5-6. What punishment do you think the majority inflicted on this man?

*When believers hurt one another now, what punishments do we administer?

This division boils down to one disappointment: As a believer, *he shouldn't have*. It's easier to forgive non-Christians when they injure us. They are unaware of godly community. But when another believer does the hurting, we are doubly stung. How can she know about mercy, kindness, and others before self and still do that? We find it incredible that Christians can be so harmful. There is often not much grace in the family that was born of grace.

But Friends, we are just people. We've been covered in Jesus' sacrifice and have the Holy Spirit, but while we walk this earth, we're susceptible to the very sins that required a Savior in the first place. Since Satan can't deny us salvation, he'll mar it with judgment, bitterness, self-righteousness, and condemnation. He capitalizes on the sins believers commit against each other—first in the injury, then in the separation.

Read 2 Corinthians 2:7-8. If this is God's plan for restoration, what do you think Satan's plan is?

When Brandon and I first began student ministry, a woman launched a campaign against my husband. It was a distorted version of truth, entirely manipulated. She worked to undermine him in the eyes of our pastor and to gain the support of other church members. It was all behind our backs while she remained kind to our faces.

We were devastated. The layers of pain went deep. We had to untangle the gossip and reclaim credibility when we'd done nothing to lose it. To say I wanted to jack her in the jaw and walk away forever is putting it sweetly. You cross me, I can find compassion. You cross my husband, you'd better duck.

A year later we accepted a position at another church.

When we announced our decision, she came to me with tears and apologized for the whole ordeal, saying, "I hope this has nothing to do with me. I really don't want you to leave."

I'd been waiting for that moment, so I thought I'd want to say, "Yes. This actually is entirely your fault. You made serving here miserable, and I hope you feel guilty," though that wasn't at all why we were leaving. But Girlfriends, God so gripped my heart with the need to forgive that I threw my arms around her neck and sobbed. I could've punished her with guilt, coldness, isolation, but what would that have done for the unity of the Spirit? For her? For me?

In that moment, something spiritual happened. My heart healed. The anger I'd fiercely guarded subsided. As Paul had instructed long ago, I comforted her. And though she had hurt me, I was the comforted one. This is counterintuitive, of course, to any kind of sense. Logically, this was a great opportunity to get even, blow a gasket. But by God's design, two believers parted ways restored rather than broken, and His family was strengthened a little that day.

*Why do you think Paul told injured believers to forgive, comfort, and reaffirm their love for the one who hurt them? Where is the sense in that?

Read 2 Corinthians 2:9-11. What picture of Satan do you get in these verses?

Satan weaves a web of deception, manipulating God's family into turning on one another. Sometimes he pits one against one: "You gossiped about me; you flirted with my husband; you lied to me." Other times he capitalizes on existing differences to set this group against that group: "They don't understand worship; we don't like their ideas; that part of the church can just leave." In fierce campaigns, he pits several against one: "We don't like you; we're over here together and you're out."

We are not unaware of his schemes.

But Satan has an ally in us. The Bible calls it our flesh, the inclination to trust anyone but God for life, fueled by thinking God's ways might not be reliable. Our flesh gives Satan's suggestions something to stick to. God's strategy against this is a strange idea: *dying* to self, sin, that wayward earthly nature.

In *Connecting*, Larry Crabb wrote,

> The Bible tells us what the fruit of our sinful nature looks like, but when we see it in our lives at a particular moment, it doesn't always look so bad. Bad urges seem reasonable, justified, necessary, even good—certainly not worthy of death. So we think about them, try to understand them, negotiate with them, find what is useful in them, and indulge them to see what happens. And we end up slaves to the flesh.[5]

What "reasonable" directions does your flesh give you for community on God's terms?

What harm do those measures actually cause?

Between a vicious Enemy, the enemy within, and a lost world, godly community is an endangered species. God's children are fragmented, isolated, and separated from each other. Satan raises a banner of victory. He's got us arguing, gossiping, harboring grudges, judging, criticizing, pretending, manipulating, and competing with each other. Meanwhile, the treasures of community are lost. There is no space for love when gossip consumes our time. When our relational reserves are poisoned, there is nothing left for the lost. We become distracted, the Enemy's special trick.

As Noam Chomsky said of conquerors, "They very naturally play upon any existing rivalries and hostilities to get one group to work for them against others. . . . That's the way conquerors work. They've always worked that way." There is no need to attack God's family from the outside if it crumbles from the inside out.

Girls, the divide-and-conquer strategy works only when we allow ourselves to be divided. Let's link arms, our diverse arms, and refuse to walk into Satan's trap. He's looking to capitalize on our differences. Let's insist they don't get the spotlight.

> In all these things *we are more than conquerors* through him who loved us. (Romans 8:37)

Which side are you helping out? Ask God to show you any ways you are harming the community of Christ. Pray for the inclinations of the flesh to be shown for what they are.

Kings, Queens, and You

Between my parents and grandparents, I learned the following growing up:

- If it tastes bad, add more butter.
- If someone waits .02 seconds after the light turns green, honk.
- If Mom says no, ask Dad.
- Remember to ask Dad first.
- Blaring gospel music is a good way to get teenagers out of bed.
- Running with a pillow apparently can put an eye out.
- If dinner burns, call it Cajun and make everyone eat it anyway.
- If you threaten your daughter by telling her she's "skating on thin water," the moment of discipline will be ruined.

Now, this isn't all I learned, but they're some of the lessons that stuck. I'm sure my family will love seeing their legacy boiled down to these nuggets, but what are they going to do?

They are welcome to write a rebuttal.

It has become clear to me how significantly our child-hoods affect our adulthoods. I once dismissed that discussion as psychobabble. I mean, enough with our moms and dads! Save your therapy money and go to Vegas. Buy yourself some happiness already. The problem is that every adult I know with relationship misery learned his or her patterns as a child. Girls, we acquired entire life models before we got out of elementary school.

Do you know God mentioned parents twenty-eight times in His Word, but He spoke of children 410 times?[6] Friends, God is fiercely pro-children. He repeatedly urges us to live well for our children's sake, to obey Him for our children's sake, to teach about Him for their sake. He is highly concerned about the childhood experience; any fool can hear His urgency. God knows that a wounded child becomes a wounded adult, so He begs us to care deeply for our little ones.

What kind of mother did you have (compassionate, distant, harsh, nurturing, overprotective . . .)?

What kind of father did you have (cold, strong, engaged, absent, hurtful . . .)?

Read Isaiah 49:13-16. *The Message* says,

Heavens, raise the roof! Earth, wake the dead!
    Mountains, send up cheers!
God has comforted his people.
    He has tenderly nursed his beaten-up, beaten-
        down people.

But Zion said, "I don't get it. GOD has left me.
     My Master has forgotten I even exist."

"Can a mother forget the infant at her breast,
     walk away from the baby she bore?
But even if mothers forget,
     I'd never forget you — never.
Look, I've written your names on the backs of my
     hands.
     The walls you're rebuilding are never out of my
     sight."

*Has a sad childhood made you cry, "The Lord has forgotten me"? What happened?

What makes a mother's lack of compassion so devastating to daughters?

In *We Are Sisters*, Dee Brestin wrote, "Women who've been blessed with a nurturing mother are likely to have rewarding friendships all of their lives. Daughters who had a cold mother, or a mother who related poorly to friends herself, have a harder climb ahead of them."[7] Some of us are imitating the very behaviors we hated growing up. That's not a stab, Girls. It's terribly hard to break the unhealthy patterns of our parents. Some never do. Those who manage to must work relentlessly.

Some of us learned that any conflict, even simple disagreement, would result in a withdrawal of love. In *Boundaries*, Henry Cloud and John Townsend explain,

When parents detach from a misbehaving young child instead of staying connected and dealing with the problem, God's constant love is misrepresented. When parents pull away in hurt, disappointment, or passive rage, they are sending this message to their young-ster: *You're loveable when you behave. You aren't love-able when you don't behave.* The child translates that message into something like this: *When I'm good, I am loved. When I'm bad, I'm cut off.*[8]

This can show up subtly through a parent's hurt tone of voice or long silence, or overtly through crying spells, illness, yelling, or complete hostility.

 How do you think this child will behave in rela-tionships when she grows up?

Others of us learned that limits were for other children, and we developed a sense of entitlement. This parenting style was the opposite of hostility. No boundaries were set; no disci-pline was enforced. We got whatever we demanded, and if we didn't right away, we threw a hissy fit until we did.

We rarely took responsibility for anything. Mom did everything around the house. Dad paid for everything. They both cleaned up our mistakes nice and neat, or they looked the other way. In doing so, they short-circuited our character development and maturity process. We learned that others' needs are secondary and the world revolves around us. If it doesn't, something is obviously wrong with the world.

 How do you think a child of these parents will behave in relationships when she grows up?

In *Safe People*, Cloud and Townsend wrote,

Entitlement destroys safety, because no normal human can fulfill our demands! It's impossible to love an entitled person, as some fault, empathic misstep, or insensitivity will send the entire relationship tumbling down. The entitled person must be listened to and understood perfectly at all times, or she feels injured and wounded.[9]

This is a learned behavior that translates to adulthood. How would it not?

The lessons we learned go on: Yelling is more effective than talking. It's better to ignore the real issues and settle for superficial ones because someone might get uncomfortable. Listening is for suckers. If people have a different opinion, browbeat them until they concede to yours. Or distance yourself from them. People who are supposed to love you will leave you, or else they'll hurt you horribly. You can't trust anyone. Women should control their environment or they'll be run over. Children should be seen and not heard. This family will appear perfect at all costs.

List the most unhealthy relationship patterns or lessons you learned growing up.

*How are those lessons affecting your relationships today? Try to be honest.

Some of you suffered terribly as little girls. Friend, if you endured abuse or neglect, if you were abandoned or verbally destroyed, I beg you to seek Christian counseling. Ignoring or denying childhood wounds will never help them heal. You'll stay a wounded mom, a wounded wife, a wounded friend. God has ordained counselors with gifts of healing, and they can help you begin the process of restoration.

We serve a God who is a Healer, a Father, a Comforter, a Restorer. It's His specialty. He is uniquely close to the broken-hearted. He is capable of breaking the cycle in your life if you'll let Him. He's no intruder; God must be invited into your brokenness. He can teach you what healthy relationships look like, and He can restore intimacy into the very places it seems unrecoverable.

Read Isaiah 49:19-21. What you are capable of producing will be too big for the cramped space you live in now! What is God showing you about breaking unhealthy cycles? What can He do?

The restoration of God is so complete it's astonishing. On the front side of it, we'd deem it impossible. We've been this way too long. Healthy relationships are a pipe dream. We enjoy our emotional barricades; they keep us safe. Yet when we allow Him to work, we look around asking, "How did this get so good? Where have these healthy relationships come from? I thought I was forgotten."

Girlfriends, your parents may have damaged you; they might have crippled your functionality. But God can make royalty out of any mess. He stands ready to rescue you. Do you understand what I am saying? Not someone else. Not her. You. He is able. He is mighty and powerful and strong. God overcomes sin and pain and damage *every single day*. It's what He does.

Read Isaiah 49:22-25. Precious, precious. What does God mean when He says, "Kings will be your foster fathers"?

*What is He showing you about any damage you sustained as a little girl? About your family now?

Sweet Friend, you may have had an absent dad, but in God's care, kings will be your foster fathers. Your mother may have been cold, but He will bring queens to be your nurturing mothers. God can prop your own children on the shoulders of warriors; the cycle need not pass to them. You are not captive to your childhood. God can rescue you from the prison that has held you. He Himself will contend for your honor, your esteem. Believer, He will save your children. They can know safe intimacy.

This is our God.

This is how He restores.

> "Then all mankind will know
>   that I, the LORD, am your Savior,
>   your Redeemer, the Mighty One of Jacob."
>   (Isaiah 49:26)

Ask God to help you break any unhealthy cycles you learned as a little girl. Pray for the strength to let Him go back there with you. Ask the Spirit to show you what it looks like to be restored.

Dig In: Thoughts from Jesus

The fifth day of each week is a time for you to be in the Word with the Holy Spirit. I won't tell random stories or teach my favorite stuff. You'll just be in Scripture. Anyone around me for half a second knows that my passion is God's Word. Packaged Bible studies are great, but God's Word is enough. Jesus prayed, "*Your word* is the truth. So let this truth make them completely yours" (John 17:17, CEV).

The best way I've found to interact with the Bible is through journaling. STAY WITH ME! Not silly diary entries or lengthy rants but a place to respond to God. His Word is His voice to us. Writing becomes our tool for talking back. We work through Scripture deliberately, with the Holy Spirit teaching us as we go. Journaling is the gift of time, time the Spirit can use to stretch our understanding, deepen our insight, and make His Word personal. It requires us to consider a verse longer than the five seconds it took to read it.

Journal however you want. Some girls write full-sentence, full-paragraph journal entries. Others write fragmented sentences in bullet points. There is no wrong way to journal through Scripture. It's a place to be honest, be angry, be thankful, ask questions. Let your understanding expand through the writing process. The Spirit is an exceptional teacher. Better than any you've ever experienced, this I promise.

I'll take you through a passage in sections. I've included several starter questions under each section. *This is not a list of questions to answer.* They're included to show you how to ask healthy questions of Scripture. Use them as a model. Work through one or two in your journal, or let the Spirit lead you differently. Fantastic Bible study is all about asking good questions.

We've already read during this week some of Jesus' prayer just before His crucifixion. Let's spend more time on it today to see how passionately Jesus felt about community.

Ask the Holy Spirit to lead you through His Word. Ask Him to teach you in whatever ways He wants to. Then read John 17:20-26 straight through. Work through each section below in your journal, focusing on the questions the Spirit brings to mind.

Read John 17:20-21.

- This part of Jesus' prayer was for future believers. See also Hebrews 7:23-25 and 1 John 2:1. How do you feel about Jesus praying for you on this very day? How must He feel about you to intercede for you like this?
- What did Jesus mean when He said "that all of them may be one"? What does that look like? How do we live as one when we're so different?
- Jesus likened our unity to the communion shared between Him and God. What kind of intimacy do They share? How can that translate to our relationships?

- How critical is it that we remain in fellowship with Jesus and the Father? How does this hold the entire mechanism together?

Read John 17:22-23.

- Jesus said the glory He gave us enables us to be one as He and God are one. What does that mean? What glory has He given us, and how does that translate to unity?
- How does our unity affect the world around us? Jesus mentioned the world fifteen times in this short prayer (17:1-16). What is His priority?
- How are we *brought* to complete unity? What is the process? Where does it begin? How does it progress?

Read John 17:24-26.

- Again Jesus references His glory from God. God gave Him this glory out of love, and Jesus has given it to us (verse 22). How is love the ultimate factor in all this?
- Jesus said the people knew Him, but they didn't know God as well as they knew Jesus. How well do you really know Jesus? God? Are They friends to you? How would you describe your relationship?
- The more we know about God, the more His love for Jesus resides in us. What do you make of this? How do we experience God's love for His Son?
- What picture of unity does Jesus close His prayer with? Draw this out if it helps you visualize Jesus' desire for unity.

Believer, if you came away with nothing else this week, I hope you caught how important community is to God. It is one of the primary reasons Jesus died. In fact, in the original language, "I want" in verse 24 means "I will that." In other words, this is Jesus' last will and testament. This represents our Savior's final and deepest wishes. When it came to His own torture, He prayed, "Not what I will, but what you will" (Mark 14:36). Yet when it came to His followers, He had a very definite will, a will that urged us toward togetherness on the deepest levels.

Don't you believe He knew something? Surely there was a reason for Jesus to hammer this so intensely. We've so talked ourselves out of vulnerable unity that it seems merely optional, even foolish. We've cornered off into sects, denominations, and divisions, and within those we hide behind pasted smiles, busyness, pretense. Unity has been diluted to a comfortable fraction of what it was intended to be. And we've declared that good enough.

If we love Jesus at all, if His death is valued whatsoever, let's join hands and run into the arms of community. Outside of loving Him and knowing the Father, it was Jesus' greatest desire. It is not good for man to be alone. Will you believe God's design more than the conventional wisdom that says "protect yourself"? Will you try? A difficult journey stretches ahead. Falsehood must be put off. Honesty has to be worn like a shield, even when it becomes uncomfortable. Barriers must come down; they aren't protective but a prison of isolation. Jesus would never lead us wrong.

Will you trust Him?

Truth or Dare

It Is Always Best to Tell the Truth

When I was twelve I walked to the gift store up the street to have a gander. As I wandered through the aisles, I spotted a stuffed dog that I had to immediately possess. There was no way to go on living without it. It cost fifteen dollars, which I did not have, as saving has never been my strong suit.

But my sister Lindsay had it.

As the oldest sister, I had a degree of influence over the others. Some would call it manipulation, but let's not split hairs. I explained to Lindsay the importance of giving me her money. There was really no other place for her savings than putting it toward my new favorite object. She saw the light and handed over her bank.

While I was fawning over my new treasure, my mom asked where it came from. Something inside told me, "You're a selfish girl who conned her little sister out of her savings," but what came out was, "I bought it with my money that I've been saving so diligently." I can't imagine why, but Mom's Bologna Radar starting going off, and she did some investigating around the house.

She did the angry walk into my room five minutes later, armed with the truth, and announced my punishment: Write, "It is always best to tell the truth" five hundred times. A smart girl would've finished in an hour, but it took this melodramatic girl six days. Mom saved the pages, and anytime I tout my merits as an excellent oldest sister, out they come as highly condemning evidence to the contrary.

It is always best to tell the truth.

Is it? Is it really? What about when the truth is ugly? What about when the truth is embarrassing? Nasty? Mean as the Devil? *Truth* is defined as "conformity with fact or reality; actuality."[1] Frankly, sometimes I don't like what is actual. Actual is yuck. I can create something much prettier than actual.

*Do you tend to acknowledge truth or deny it? How long have you done that?

Truth has been mistaken as an enemy for centuries because truth can't be manipulated and stay truth. It is what it is. If it's horrible, it's horrible. If it's humiliating, it's humiliating. You can't spin truth without losing its essence. Who I actually am, what is actually happening, is hard to accept. I so want to be a certain person with a certain life. I want less of this and more of that, but the way I really am just ruins everything.

Cloud and Townsend wrote, "We need to know, am I good or bad? We all have a problem in this area. We weren't intended to be bad, but in many ways we are. Coming to terms with badness involves great loss and struggle for us."[2] And it does. We lose the dream of the ideal. God set His character in our hearts, so we long for what's right. We wish for it. We reach for it. But we come up short, and we hate it.

Truth is brutal for me to accept.

But it's easy for Jesus.

Read John 1:14. What was Jesus like when He came to us? What picture of Him do you get from this verse? Try to unpack the meaning of *grace* and *truth* in your own words.

This is so important: Jesus came *full* of grace and truth. He wasn't 80 percent truth, 20 percent grace. Not 75 percent, 25 percent. He came 100 percent committed to truth and 100 percent committed to grace. Grace and truth. Truth and grace. Jesus knew that the people He was coming for were a mess. He knew we would lie, cheat, betray, fall away. He understood the battle in our hearts between what we want to be and what we are. Jesus knew the truth.

And He never shrank from it. He told the Samaritan woman at the well, "*The fact is*, you have had five husbands, and the man you now have is not your husband" (John 4:18). Jesus told His disciples after his encounter with the rich young man, "*I tell you the truth*, it is hard for a rich man to enter the kingdom of heaven" (Matthew 19:23). He told His disciples before His crucifixion, "*I tell you the truth*, one of you will betray me" (Matthew 26:21). It was all true.

Jesus often shares hard truth with me: "You are acting selfishly. You are too concerned with what others think of you. You treated her ugly, and it hurt her. You're ignoring Me. I want to work on this area, and you're not cooperating. It's going to come back and bite you."

When Jesus communicates truth about you, what does He say?

*What is true in your life that you hate?

And here is where we get stuck. We hear the facts we already know, and we shut down. We lock up in shame and learn to hate the truth. Even as Christ-followers, we still struggle, sin, and fail. No amount of willpower and church attendance will change that. The best Christian you know, the one who would *never* do what you did, sins. Her selfish nature sometimes wins out. So does yours. So does mine. This is truth. It has always been true, and it will be until Jesus comes back.

God is not surprised or horrified. He long ago came up with a solution for His fallen human race. He saw how we actually were and sent a perfect Savior to bridge the gap. This perfect Jesus came full of truth, eyes wide open to what He was getting into. He could see every disappointment, each betrayal, and every last flaw that His sacrifice would not eradicate. He saw good intentions that wouldn't be realized. He was aware of the damage we'd incur early and repeat later. He knew we'd try as hard as we could and fail.

So He came full of grace.

Read John 1:16-17. Have you experienced the *fullness* of Jesus' grace? If so, how? If not, what do you suppose is getting in the way?

*How do you (or don't you) reconcile truth with grace?

If the law through Moses is on one side and Jesus' grace and truth is on the other, where are you living? On the effort-based, rigid side of the law, or on the forgiving, compassionate side of grace and truth?

Girlfriends, Jesus looks at us with eyes of truth. There is nothing hidden. And then He opens His arms and says, "Come. I love you today." We don't have to be good to be loved. That was never part of the deal. Grace is unearned, thank goodness. He can reconcile what is true about us with His mercy. The two don't conflict.

It's time to make peace with truth. Let's no longer be enemies. If Jesus can face the truth of you, of your life, it's safe for you to do so. Being angry at the truth isn't helpful. Pretending it doesn't exist isn't either. Cloud and Townsend said, "People who can't reconcile either their own or anyone else's faults suffer tremendous isolation because they are unable to attach to real, whole people who are both good *and* bad. The ideals of what 'should' be get in the way."[3]

How does "should" show up in your life? Your history? Your current choices? Your personality? Other people? How is it keeping you from grace?

Jesus stands shoulder to shoulder with you, looking at the truth. It's not you on one side and Him on the other. He doesn't declare, "I'm disappointed." He says, "Let's you and Me get busy on this." It's a roll-up-our-sleeves approach: "We can handle this together. I'll love you the same every single second of it." That is grace, Girls. It is not condemning, nor is it permissive. It's altogether loving, and it's not put off by truth. In fact, it can only be realized once truth is faced.

Grace and truth are best friends. In fact, the corresponding Hebrew terms are often translated *unfailing love* and *faithfulness*, and as the psalmist reminds us,

> Love and faithfulness meet together;
> righteousness and peace kiss each other.
> (Psalm 85:10)

Truth is the front door to the warm, inviting home of grace. You can't know the second without embracing the first.

So we can't go on without making friends with truth in general. It is the foundation for every healthy relationship. It's nothing to be scared of. Jesus would tell you it's nothing to be ashamed of either. A woman ready to be truthful is a real commodity. That's when Jesus rubs His kind hands together and says, "Excellent! Let's get going. We can finally move forward."

From the fullness of his grace we have all received one blessing after another. (John 1:16)

How is your relationship with truth? Ask the Spirit to help you face it honestly. Pray for a spirit of grace to win out. It can. That's a gift from Jesus.

Lies We Tell Ourselves

I recently had a speaking engagement at a gi-normous church. They needed one hundred volunteers just to direct cars in the parking lot. From the second they asked me to give the Sunday morning message, I stopped sleeping. I fretted. I obsessed over my talk. I went way over my grace limit on an outfit. I became oblivious to anyone else's needs for two weeks.

That Sunday morning in my hotel, I tried to talk myself out of raging nerves: "You are calm. This is no big deal. It's the tiniest deal you've ever seen. In fact, you're having fun. This is fun. You love this part. You are confident. You are like a piece of iron. Platinum, really. You're strong like a diamond. You're basically a wedding ring."

Yet as I put my mascara on, my hands were shaking and both my eyelids were twitching. I looked like a deranged schizo in pretty clothes. My pep talk to myself had no real effect, regardless of how much I wanted it to.

See, I was scared, so I lied to myself.

My Girlfriends in Christ, many of us are petrified of real community. The notion is so terrifying that we tell ourselves a nice series of lies to keep our distance. We play mental games with ourselves to keep us safe, far from the authenticity of true friendship.

*When you think of honest, raw relationships with other women, do you have any fears (big or small)?

This fear must be faced because it is the catalyst for pretending. Fear begins circumstantially: "She hurt me; I was embarrassed; they judged me." But when left unattended, it becomes an identity. We form protective layers around our fear until it becomes absorbed into our spirit, as much a part of us as our beating hearts. From that place, we interact with the rest of humanity in a fragmented, fake manner.

To justify such pretending, we have to do a little two-step. Truth would expose our fear as unhealthy, so we rationalize it instead. In *Why Am I Afraid to Tell You Who I Am?* John Powell said, "Very often there are two reasons for everything we do: the alleged good reason and the real reason. We make our emotional preferences our rational conclusions. Rationalization is the bridge that makes my wishes the facts. It is the use of intelligence to deny the truth; it makes us dishonest with ourselves."[4]

Inner Lie #1: I don't really need anyone else.

Read Colossians 2:1-5. What benefits of love and unity did Paul explain?

Paul said their unity was his reason for writing to this young church: "My purpose is that they may be encouraged in heart and united in love" (verse 2). These are the words of a wise man. His letters went to whole churches. His heartbeat was for community. Wisdom, understanding, the treasures of

Christ — none are possible outside togetherness. There is no such thing as a healthy spiritual island.

Cloud and Townsend wrote, "God has created all of us incomplete, inadequate, and in need of a huge shopping list full of ingredients that we cannot provide ourselves. Yet we desire to be a universe unto ourselves. We resist admitting we can't make it on our own, that we don't have it together. We do not want to admit our impoverishment, because it's humiliating."[5]

As Paul wrote, many fine-sounding arguments deceive us toward autonomy: "I'm really doing fine. I truly don't need other women in my life. I am strong and independent. I have my husband, and that's enough." These lies stick because our culture equates self-sufficiency with maturity. We see that as an admirable quality. Needy, hurting people are faith deficient, no doubt. We talk ourselves out of loneliness and rationalize our superficiality, all in the name of "I don't need you."

Is this you? What fine-sounding arguments do you tell yourself about needing other women?

In this case, we are also forced to tell ourselves that we're above correction. We can't receive it if we won't admit our need for it. We are above nurturing. We are above tenderness. We are above the wisdom of other women. Our sins are inconsequential. Our behavior is always above reproach. We are such exceptional mothers, wives, and people that it is unnecessary to invite friends into those places. They're never broken.

Inner Lie #2: I don't want you deeply in my life.

Read some of Paul's words to the Colossians in 1:3-4,9; 2:1,5 again; and 4:7-9. How would you describe Paul's tone? What do you hear?

Paul's affection is legendary. We never hear any self-sufficient attitude, any I-could-take-you-or-leave-you sentiments. He practically dripped with overt love for his friends. He was always saying, "I wish I were with you; I think of you constantly; I miss you; you are so dear to me." He let the bonds of friendship take deep root in his heart. He embraced every hug, every kiss, every extension of love his friends offered, and he returned it tenfold.

In order to stave off fear and protect our hearts, we convince ourselves that we not only don't need other women but, by golly, we don't want them either. You know what we say: "Women are catty. They're too complicated. They'll talk about me the second I go to the bathroom. I gave up drama when I was in sixth grade." Then we play "what if" and make up in our heads awful scenarios fueled by paranoia.

Is this you? If so, what is your alleged reason for not *wanting* other women deeply in your life?

Is there a real reason under that defensiveness?

Henri Nouwen said, "The real danger facing us is to distrust our desire for communion. It is a God-given desire without which our lives lose their vitality and our hearts grow cold."[6] Friend, the desire for deep relationship is there. It's why every little girl's greatest fear is being left out. It's why we engineer sleepovers for our daughters with an even number of friends. But when that desire is crushed long enough, the protective layers form, and we toss our hair back defiantly: "I don't want you."

But the desire remains, even if we pretend it doesn't.

Girls, to crave the joys of friendship is *godly*. It is looking Jesus in the eye and telling Him, "You were right about community." Anytime we want for our lives what God does, we can expect heaven's stamp of approval. In fact, *confession* is defined as "saying the same thing as." In other words, when we say the same thing about our sin as God does, we are in confession. So when we say the same thing about our need for community as God does, we're confessing that His plans are trustworthy.

Inner Lie #3: Being vulnerable would be catastrophic.

This is another version of the "what if" game. If I said how I really feel, everything would go to hell in a handbasket. If I said I was struggling, our entire social infrastructure would come crashing down. If I admitted my sin issues, I'd set off a judgment frenzy. The phones would be ringing around my neighborhood for weeks. What would they think of my husband? What would they think of my kids? What would they think of me?

It would be terrible.

Bill Hybels calls this one of the five deadly lies. He wrote,

> We all have our list of phrases that trip our truth-detector button. . . . There is a spirit of error in this world. There is also a spirit of truth. We've all been burned by the spirit of error before, so we need to stay alert. When certain phrases trip our truth sensors, we need to raise our consciousness and prepare ourselves for action. . . . When we are anxious about what might happen, what people might think, or how terrible the results will be, we are buying into a deadly lie.[7]

Is this you? What do you think would be so terrible about being vulnerable with other women?

Friend, would it? Would it really be that terrible? If you admitted your struggle with anger, would anyone die? If you told a group of safe women, "I need you," would you become a pariah? The Enemy works with our insecurities and exaggerates the results of any given action. He embellishes the consequences and uses our own paranoia to generate fear. He'll use whatever he can to keep us from the power of real community.

The lie is not true.

 Read Colossians 2:8. What principles of this world take you captive when you buy into this inner lie?

*Paul called these lies hollow and deceptive. Do you see any negative consequences to living like this?

Remember the church I was speaking at? Land sakes, I was terrified. But know this: My girlfriends prayed for weeks for me. A set of friends drove to Houston to be cheerleaders. My Girlfriends Christi and Stephanie offered to write "Go Jen" on their bras and unbutton their shirts in the sanctuary. We decided that was unnecessary. My best friends from Corpus Christi came instead of going to a family reunion. My neighbors sent out mass e-mails. My phone rang off the hook all weekend with friends calling to say, "You go, girl." Those closest to me saw me through.

I needed them.

I wanted them.

Catastrophe would've been being alone.

What lies are you telling yourself in this area? Ask the Spirit of truth to reign in your heart. Pray for the lies to be exposed. You don't want to be your own worst enemy.

Lies We Tell God

You know when God makes a big list of sins and then tells us to steer clear of them? Like, "We also know that law is made not for the righteous but for lawbreakers and rebels, the ungodly and sinful, the unholy and irreligious; for those who kill their fathers or mothers, for murderers, for adulterers and perverts, for slave traders and liars and perjurers—and for whatever else is contrary to the sound doctrine" (1 Timothy 1:9-10). I used to scan that list, thinking, *Those people are a mess*. The Pharisees and I would have gotten along just fine, clearly.

So it was distressing to discover that I'm actually on that list. I haven't killed my parents or traded slaves, per se. I've never cheated on my husband, as I'm profaithfulness. I'm not really a lawbreaker, unless speeding counts.

But I am a liar.

I used to think of liars as those who made up crazy stories and tricked people, the ones who ended up on *Dateline* and behind bars. The bad liars, if you will. But I've learned that I lie, too. I lie all the time.

To God.

Yesterday we looked at three lies we tell ourselves about real friendship. Today we'll study two lies we tell God. After all, we have to keep a united front if we're going to remain safe in isolation.

How would you describe your communication with God? Raw? Formal and stiff? Brutally honest? Awkward? Tender?

I'm a PK (pastor's kid), so I'm altogether familiar with churchy language. I know the right words to say, the right way to worship, the right comments to make, the right prayers to deliver. I've heard them for thirty years. But I've learned that many of them are utterly false. There is no place more fake these days than the church. I'm sick of it. God is sick of it. He would prefer an honest mess over a pretty lie every day of the week.

Lie to God #1: I believe You.

We say this all the time—in our songs, in our prayers, in our commentary: "You are good, God. You love us, God. You are so smart, God. We believe it. We really do. Go, God! Yeah, Jesus! We believe in You, too. We are believers. Believe You me."

But how different would our lives look if we really believed Him?

If we really believed He was right about honest relationships, wouldn't everything be different from how it is now? Believing *in* God is one thing. Believing Him is another. Yes, we know that God said healing comes from confessing our sins to each other, but we don't believe it or else we'd do it. Healing should be private. Nice try, God. Sure, He told us that honesty is like a kiss on the lips, but we're not sure He was right. Honesty makes people uncomfortable. God must have gotten confused.

But we believe you, God. Just listen and we'll tell You.

Read Ecclesiastes 5:1-3. Why would God prefer our silence over our hasty declarations of belief?

*Regarding community, do you have a hard time believing God? What do you tell Him?

Matthew Henry wrote, "Thoughts are words to God, and words are but wind if they be not copied from the thoughts."[8] We try to flatter God, but He wasn't born yesterday. Solomon begged us not to make the sacrifice of fools with our false announcements of belief. Girls, false sacrifices are simply no sacrifices. I believe You, but I couldn't sacrifice my pride. I believe You, but I refuse to sacrifice my fear. I believe You, but I can't sacrifice my image, my family's image.

I believe You, but I really don't.

If you really believed God, what would you have to sacrifice?

Sweetest Friends, God's Word tells us otherwise: "From the beginning God chose you to be saved through the sanctifying work of the Spirit and *through belief in the truth*" (2 Thessalonians 2:13). When we choose God's truth over fear, over pride, the Spirit blesses us and makes us holy. When you obey in belief, even though you're terrified, He breaks the shackles from your feet. God can lead you only to the truth, and the truth will set you free. Believe that.

Lie to God #2: I feel _____ about community.

This is usually a lie of omission. "Let's talk about service, God, maybe some parenting issues. I'm right as rain on the subjects of temptation, spiritual gifts, Bible history, Moses. That Moses sure was a character, wasn't he, Jesus? Let's talk about him." We skim over the Scriptures that call us to radical community. We ignore those. We think by staying spiritually busy with other parts of God's Word, we are exempt from a primary theme of the New Testament.

Yet God tells us we were created to thrive in relationships with other believers. It's the only way. So pretending to be healthy in the absence of community requires us to play games with God. It offers Him the safe parts of our lives while pretending He can't see this one. Consequently, it eliminates all guidance from Him that has to do with community.

Help me with my marriage, God.	*Let My people surround you.*
I'm failing as a mom, Lord.	*Let My wise ones counsel you.*
I'm struggling with depression.	*Find healing in My church.*

Do you make this part of your life available to God, or do you pretend it doesn't exist?

*How might God want to use community in your biggest struggle right now?

Girlfriends, it's okay to be honest with God. We can tell Him how we feel about this whole thing. Your silence may be better than your dishonesty, but your truthfulness is infinitely better than your silence. Maybe you need to say:

- I've never been open. I learned to pretend when I was little. Honesty with other women is so far beyond me that I don't even know how to begin, God.
- The thought of anyone knowing what goes on in my head is more than I can bear, Lord. Why do we have to be honest? I don't want to be.
- I'm angry that You've asked me to be vulnerable, God. You know how that has hurt me in the past. I'm not sure I can do it.
- I can't get past the "what ifs," Jesus. I can't see that the benefits will outweigh the consequences.

God doesn't hear a true feeling and get angry. A foolish sacrifice? Save it. A hasty promise? Spare Him. An honest emotion? Now we're getting somewhere. He can work with a woman who faces the truth. And PS: He already knows how you feel, so there's really no point in pretending. You're as convincing as my poor husband was when I remembered at 7:00 p.m. that it was his birthday yesterday and he told me he was "fine" with my utter neglect. Bless him.

What would you honestly say to God about your feelings on this subject?

These lies to God ultimately mean we live a false life unto Him. "I'm Your girl, God. I'm all about living for You. But only in the areas I'm interested in." There are parts of a godly life we love and parts we could do without. So we approach His Word like a spiritual buffet, picking and choosing our favorite dishes. We'll take that salvation, thanks. We'll have a helping of that good forgiveness. Love that. Blessings? Yes. Mercy? Absolutely.

Real community? Pass.

David gave an example of the way we should respond to this kind of God:

> I am under vows to you, O God;
>   I will present my thank offerings to you.
> For you have delivered me from death
>   and my feet from stumbling,
> that I may walk before God
>   in the light of life. (Psalm 56:12-13)

For all we've received, God asks only for our love, our belief evidenced by our choices.

Read Ecclesiastes 5:4-7. The opposite of fulfilling our vow to God is meaningless words spoken to Him. You'll never be perfect, but how are you doing in fulfilling your vows to the One who saved you?

Girls, God will never lead you wrong. It is safe to be faithful to a faithful God. He tells us that lies are the native tongue of Satan. The Enemy tried to convince the first woman that God's ways couldn't be trusted: "*Did God really say*, 'You must not eat from any tree in the garden'?" (Genesis 3:1). He whispers to you:

> *Did God really say*, "Make every effort to keep the unity of the Spirit"?
> *Did God really say*, "The whole body is joined and held together by each supporting ligament"?
> *Did God really say*, "Love each other as I have loved you"?
> *Did God really say*, "Boast of the things that show your weakness"?

Girlfriends, God's ways can be trusted. We can believe Him. And if we can't, we can move in that direction until we do. He will ultimately win us over with truth. Let's put the lies behind us: those we tell ourselves and those we tell God. How about we start over from the place of raw confession? "This is how I feel. This is where I am. This is what I believe. This is what I can't quite believe. There You go, God. That's what You have to work with."

He who conceals his sins does not prosper,
but whoever confesses and renounces them finds
mercy. (Proverbs 28:13)

 Have you been flattering God? Get honest before Him today. Say every true thing you've been hiding.

Zacchaeus Was a Wee Little Man

Indulge me if you will with one more day on honesty (as if you have a choice). Forget being truthful with other people; that's next week. We're still working on being honest with ourselves and then with God. There's no point in moving forward until we stop lying to those two. So I'll show you what getting real with Jesus looks like. Thank goodness we have the Word, or we might leave this confrontation up to our imaginations, and you know how they exaggerate.

After three years of ministry primarily in northern Galilee, Jesus set His sights on Jerusalem, the preappointed place of His death. His hour had come. He began the journey with His disciples, making the most of every opportunity along the way. When He was passing through Jericho, fifteen miles east of Jerusalem, He made a special stop. With barely one week left to live, He deemed this encounter worthy of His final days.

*Read Luke 19:1-2. Jesus was out of time, yet He stopped for one man's soul. What does this tell you about Jesus?

Jericho boasted over ten thousand priests, but none of them turned Jesus' head.[9] Of all the likely recipients of Jesus' final hours, a chief tax collector was not one. Basically a turncoat, this Jewish man collected taxes for the Romans who governed their land. That betrayal was bad enough, but it was common knowledge that tax collectors also charged more than was owed the Romans and pocketed the difference. They were card-carrying extortionists who profited from the Roman occupation the Jews detested.

And Zacchaeus was the *chief* tax collector at that. Luke was sure to tell us of his wealth. So he not only cheated the Jewish people, but he also took a cut from the tax collectors under him. No one would have cried if Zacchaeus got hit by a chariot.

Read Luke 19:3-4. What do you see in Zacchaeus here?

Under our sins, our poor decisions, our selfishness, there is usually tenderness, too. The authors of *TrueFaced* wrote, "Although we may have accumulated titles, status, and accomplishments, we personally remain wounded and immature—long on 'success,' but short on dreams. We admire people who live the TrueFaced life, but our loss of hope has forced us into desperately trying to discover safety from behind our masks. In a very real sense, we are *all* performers."[10]

Like Zacchaeus, we want to see Jesus. We've heard about His gentleness, how He loves the unlovable. People say there is no sin He's unwilling to forgive. Others seem to have been downright rescued by His mercy. But there's a hitch: We're not certain if it's safe to get real with Him. Once He hears all we've done, the thoughts in our heads, well, the wheels could come right off. We've got some real issues. We've done some bad stuff. Sure, Jesus loves the widows and orphans, but we might be more than He's willing to deal with.

So maybe we'll check Him out from a distance. Our hearts burn to get a glimpse, one touch of His hand. The life we're living has left us parched, but it's the life we know. It's the life everyone else knows we live. Showing our cards is more than we can imagine. We need to keep a safe space between us—but wouldn't it be astonishing if He was who He said He was?

What if it's true?

*Do you ever feel like Zacchaeus? Curious but ashamed? Desperate but scared? How do you feel about a face-to-face encounter with Jesus?

Read Luke 19:5-7. How do you think the other Jews wanted Jesus to feel about Zacchaeus?

Of all the people Jesus could've loved that day, doesn't it seem strange that He'd choose a man who oppressed His people? Jesus was usually against those who hurt His nation. The Pharisees? Forget about it. The officials? Silent treatment. He had harsh words for the pious and self-righteous. Jesus loved the downtrodden, the brokenhearted. He was never about the greatest, always the least.

Yet today, He didn't stop for a widow, a leper, the sick, or the dying. He stopped for a Roman accomplice who cheated the Jews for a fat profit. And there was no rebuke, no lecture on Zacchaeus's behavior. Jesus only called him by name and closed the gap Zacchaeus kept between them. "Come out of that tree, closer to Me. I'm coming to your house. *I must*."

What must Jesus have known about Zacchaeus's heart?

Sweet Friend, it's true. Jesus *is* close to the brokenhearted.

He knows. He knows when the exterior doesn't match the pain within. He knows when outward successes mask the emptiness inside. He sees past sins and terrible choices and looks straight into the soul. He understands the factors that have contributed to the woman you are today—the disappointments, betrayals, sins of others. Your polished facade doesn't fool Jesus.

Nor does it put Him off. He's not scared of the real you. It's not scary for the real you to stand in front of Jesus, either. In Scripture, Jesus welcomed every honest sinner, no matter the sin. He loved each one fiercely. There is no condemnation from Jesus of a woman who faces her sin. None. There is no shame, no guilt. He doesn't keep a record. There is no fear or humiliation. There is only forgiveness and wholeness.

It's who Jesus is.

*Read Luke 19:8-9. Look at Zacchaeus. The first thing he was compelled to say was a confession. What must it be like to stand honestly in front of Jesus?

We think we'd want to lie, make everything seem a little better than it is. But a real encounter with Jesus shows us otherwise. To stand under Jesus' love removes all need to pretend.

See, Jesus came to seek and to save what was lost.

When we adopted our dog Texas from the pound, he was a stray. He was four, so he'd spent years lost and wandering. The day we brought him home, Texas was skin and bones, he had heartworms, and his hair was thin and matted. He was intimidated by my husband, and he buried all his food. He was a mess.

But we were intent on loving him. We gently brushed his hair, gave him the best treats. My kids petted him so often I thought they'd rub his hair off. They were in the backyard first thing in the morning and last thing at night. My husband talked sweet to him and taught him to wrestle. I let Texas lie in my lap for ear scratching, though I was supposedly the reluctant participant in dog ownership.

And he became so beautiful. His hair and body filled in, strong and healthy. He plays tag with our kids and walks perfectly on a leash now. There has never been a more affectionate dog or a family who loves their pet so much. We didn't want a purebred; we wanted to save a lost dog. But in our eyes, he's as good as pedigreed now.

Believer, Jesus knows we're lost. That's the whole point of His coming. He came to this dog pound of a world looking for the mangiest, poorest treated, most malnourished people He could find. We don't have to pretend we like wandering the streets. No need to hide our wounds or make excuses for our appearance. We just need to lay our heads in Jesus' lap and let Him love us back to health.

Can you stand before Jesus today owning your brokenness? Your lostness? Your choices? What do you need to say? What do you need to hear?

Oh, Girls, that moment of truth is worth every moment of freedom that comes after it. It's such a relief to say the worst thing about yourself and find Jesus still standing there, arms open. And here is where we begin because we learn about safe relationships. We discover the joy of being accepted. We find out that Jesus doesn't leave, nor does He condemn.

And when we experience this place of grace, we learn to extend it to our other relationships. It becomes the map by which we find our way in friendship. We learn to choose forgiveness over bitterness, compassion over selfishness, mercy over judgment, honesty over pretending. When our friendships mimic our relationship with Jesus, there is delight unheard of. We become a community of grace, a

group of strays who were once lost but have been found.
And saved.

Grace is so good, Believer. Are you ready to get real?
Ask God to show you anything that still stands in your
way.

Dig In: Reckless Trust

The rest of this study involves the nitty-gritty of friendship, and quite frankly, it's about to get bumpier. Putting God's Word into practice is always harder than thinking about it privately. So, Dear Friends, it comes down to this: Do you trust God? Do you trust His ways? Or maybe the question is, will you try? Because once we decide that He really is for us, He really is all knowing, He really is desperate for our wholeness, then it's a little easier to obey.

Anytime I'm wrestling with trust, I turn to David. He gave us such honest examples to learn from. Line by line, he worked it out with God. Sometimes he argued and other times he pleaded, but he always came back to "I trust You, Lord." Spend a few minutes in prayer asking the Spirit to search you. Pray for an encounter with reckless trust.

Open to Psalm 40 and read verses 1-8 straight through. Then go back and work through each of the following sections in your journal. Remember, this is not a list of questions to answer. Let the Spirit lead you to the ones reserved for you today.

Read Psalm 40:1-3.

- How did God rescue you? From what did He save you?
- What song has He put in your mouth? Many believers truly have a song that speaks of their relationship with God. Do you?
- Where would you be today if God had not lifted you out of your slimy pit?
- Would people look at your life and trust in God simply based on your testimony? What would they say?

Read Psalm 40:4-5.

- Do you believe the woman who trusts the Lord is blessed? Do you really believe it? Write your thoughts. Ask God to search you on this one.
- Proud people and false gods are sorry recipients of your trust. What is your experience with them?
- Look at God's wonders! He is worthy of our trust! What wonders have you seen in your life? In your circle of this world?
- We cannot even number the wonderful things God has planned for us. He needs you to go along willingly. Are you helping or hurting God's marvelous plans for you? How?

Read Psalm 40:6-8.

- Friend, God doesn't want your dutiful sacrifices. He wants to pierce your ears with the truth of Himself.

Have you tried to appease Him with works? What is He trying to tell you today?

- "Here I am, I have come." Can you tell God this? Will you believe Him? Obey Him? Stand true and present in front of Him? Pray these words to God. Tell Him.
- The woman who believes God's will is best desires to fulfill it. Are you ready? Will you commit to trust for the rest of this study? Will you release what you think you know about community and believe God instead? Talk this over with Him. Let Him help you.

I love this passage. There is no other God like this. We serve a Savior who rescues us out of sheer love and then nourishes us back to health. He begs us to trust Him because there is not one person who loves us more or has better dreams for us. He wants us in the safe harbor of His plans, protected from every lesser option. He tells us, "Believe Me because I love you. Believe Me because I would never harm you. Believe Me because I really know what brings life to you." To help our trust, God performs wonders that leave us speechless. He says, "See? This is who I am."

He doesn't want our fearful sacrifices or offerings of appeasement. He wants us to hear Him. *Hear Him finally.* God is looking for the woman who can stand at the throne and say, "Here I am, I have come."

Your trust is safe with Him, Girlfriends. Believe Him. When you hit a rough patch with forgiveness next week, believe Him when He tells you to let go. When you are faced with the choice to be honest with safe women, believe Him when He declares that the best way. If a godly confrontation is in order, believe Him when He promises restoration. Put on trust like a shield, protecting your-self against conventional wisdom and worldly rules of engagement. Become a real believer, and your life will never look the same.

> "Do not let your hearts be troubled. Trust in God; trust also in me." (John 14:1)

Where Have All the Good People Gone?

Unsafe People

The summer before my fourth-grade year we moved to another state. Sadly, this was at the height of my awkward status. I was riding the heels of a botched home perm, I wore plastic glasses from the Bargain Selection, and my scratched mosquito bites looked like leprosy. Add monstrous buck teeth and a closet full of terry cloth, and BAM! Dork alert.

In my new school, there was a group of cool girls. They wore Forenza and Outback Red, and they got their perms at the salon. I so wanted to be in their crowd, but my Nerd Factor was at an all-time high. Having no social skills, I loitered around the edges of their group, hoping to get absorbed by proximity. Little did I know I was setting myself up. Because miracle of miracles! They asked me to the movies with them. The movie choice: *Breakin'*, the coolest movie of 1984. I tried to play it cool, but I didn't really have that skill set. So I obsessed over clothes and hair and interesting things to say for a week until my grand initiation.

Come to find out, it was a big joke. Let's invite the Donkey Teeth Girl and pretend we like her! She'll play the fool, and we'll laugh about it for years. It was like a lame After School

Special, except I never got the makeover and redemption. I was just an ugly nine-year-old with Willy Wonka hair who was betrayed. (Don't feel sorry for me. I'm cute now.)

Mean girls.

Let's have it, Girlfriends—a collective sigh. We remember. We rapidly discovered that girls could be terrible. We entered this world believing all relationships were safe, but that notion quickly expired.

How old were you when you learned that girls could be terrible? What happened?

As we move forward, it's critical to evaluate the friends we'll be moving forward with. Just because Jesus heralded relationships does not mean we should cultivate intimacy with every person. Jesus wasn't an idiot. Some people are dangerous; they can't be trusted with the treasure of you. We need to recognize unsafe people when they're looking us in the face.

Cloud and Townsend summed up unsafe people by grouping them into three categories. They wrote, "We choose people based on outward appearance, and then experience the inside of them. We look at worldly success, charm, looks, humor, status and education, accomplishments, talents and giftedness, or religious activity. But then we experience the pain of being in a real relationship with them, and come up very empty-handed."[1]

Unsafe People, Type #1: Abandoners

These are the friends who start a relationship but can't finish it. They seem promising at the beginning; they are so into us. Their enthusiasm for a new relationship is almost over the top. But the second the waters get bumpy, good-bye. Many times abandoners have been abandoned themselves. They don't understand what faithful relationships look like. There's no grace for rough patches, no flexibility for real life. At one extreme, they choose only surface acquaintances because their fear of abandonment keeps them frozen. At the other extreme, they look only for perfect friends, and they leave when the relationship encounters real life.

*Read Romans 15:5-6. Why would Paul use the term *endurance* when discussing unity?

Girls, we need friends who will go the distance with us. There are times when we are messy. It won't be fun to stick with us. As astonishing as this sounds, sometimes we won't have it together. What happens when our marriage is suffering? When our kids are out of control? When we're in a dark place? That's when abandoners check out. They aren't willing to get their hands that dirty. They're suddenly unavailable when we need them. Girls, if we wanted to be dumped again, we'd call our high school boyfriends.

These are some warning signs of abandoners:

- She blames other people, her history, God, or anything else rather than taking responsibility for her life.
- She stays angry and bitter, sometimes for life.
- She's consumed with "I" instead of "you" or "we."
- She avoids closeness instead of really connecting.
- You are the giver; she is the taker.
- You feel responsible for her stability; you walk on eggshells.
- She is often a flashy, intense, addictive type who is unstable with commitments in general.
- She is unable to function in crisis.

What is your history with abandoners? Have you been left by one?

Are you an abandoner? What keeps you from sticking?

Unsafe People, Type #2: Critics

Critics take a parental role with their friends—and everyone else, for that matter. They are judgmental, speak rashly, and create little to no room for grace. Sadly, these friends are common in spiritual circles. Critics are all about the principle but neglect the need for love, mercy, or forgiveness. You will receive much condemnation from this girl, though she will package it as helpfulness. Expect nothing to be her fault and her solutions to always be right.

*Read Romans 15:7. We are to accept each other as Jesus accepted us. What does that mean? How did He accept us?

Give me a friend any day who will love me as I am. Girls, we need to be challenged, yes, but not criticized. Mutuality must be present in a thriving friendship. I love you; you love me. I'm not better than you. You're no loonier than me. When one participant is always elevated over the other, that relationship is a sham. The key idea is balance; look for shared value, shared esteem, shared respect. If we wanted another mother, we'd move back home.

These are some warning signs of critics:

- She never admits her own weaknesses.
- She cannot be confronted without responding with defensiveness.

- She is self-righteous, never humble.
- Her opinions are law and well-broadcasted.
- She does not respect your "no" or a different opinion of any kind. Instead, she withdraws emotionally, acts hurt, applies guilt, or condemns your choices.
- She sees you as inferior and treats you as such.
- You feel like a kid around her.
- You feel controlled and anxious around her; you become compliant.

Do you have a critic who masquerades as a friend? How do you respond to her?

Are you a critic? If so, what compels you to act this way?

Unsafe People, Type #3: Irresponsibles

Irresponsibles can't seem to take care of themselves or anyone else. The consequences of their actions are your problem, not theirs, and getting them to follow through is like pulling teeth. While an irresponsible friend may be super fun to be around, you simply cannot trust her. She is just not dependable. She's always late, always a mess, too unorganized to be reliable, always dropping the ball, never standing by her word, and unconcerned with how this affects you.

*Read Romans 15:8-9. To make good on a promise made earlier, Jesus became a servant of the Jews. What does this teach us about the importance of our word?

Girls, let's find friends who do what they say they'll do. We need grown-up girlfriends. We have too many kids and responsibilities to have to deal with managing someone else's unreliability. Jesus said, "Simply let your 'Yes' be 'Yes,' and your 'No,' 'No'" (Matthew 5:37). Let's surround ourselves with women whose "yes" can be trusted. A promise made is worth nothing until the promise is kept. If we wanted another kid, well, I guess we'd just birth one.

These are some warning signs of irresponsibles:

- She is often in financial crisis because of irresponsible spending.
- She needs friends who will protect her and tell her what to do.
- She avoids working on her problems rather than dealing with them.
- She will always flatter you and justify your actions rather than confront you.
- You feel like a parent with her.
- She lets you down frequently.
- You apologize to others regarding her or make excuses for her.
- You pick up her slack often.
- You resent her.

Do you have an irresponsible friend? How do you truly feel about that relationship?

Are you irresponsible? How do you think your friends feel about rescuing you all the time?

Unsafe people turn friendships into a trainwreck, Girlfriends. They make growing, mutual relationships impossible. But it takes two to tango. For every unsafe person, there is a friend allowing the behavior. We can't complain about being burned if we keep stepping into the flames.

There is no point in talking about godly community until we learn to make safe choices. Remember Jesus' advice: "Be as shrewd as snakes and as innocent as doves" (Matthew 10:16). The smart believer evaluates her inner circle and makes careful girlfriend choices. Jesus selected twelve, while sending away spiteful members of his own family. Beyond that, He welcomed three in even closer. He allowed one unsafe man into his inner circle, but only because Judas would help send Him to the cross. Jesus wouldn't waste one day on toxic relationships.

Why would you?

Pray for discernment for your current friendships, even if it's painful. Ask the Spirit to show you the toxic friends in your life. Then pray that if you are unsafe, God will show you and give you specifics. Don't despair; God can make anyone safe.

Safe People

My Thursday night Bible study is a group of girlfriends who journal through the Bible one book at a time. Besides that, we eat a lot, laugh, cry often, drink gallons of coffee, pray, learn, and grow together. We've met every week for three years.

I began to notice that when new girls would join us, there wasn't the normal trial period until they felt comfortable. When we hardly knew their names, girls would share volumes on their marriages, children, life heartaches. Our new Girlfriend Mary Lauren said, "I'm totally together everywhere but here; I seem to cry every Thursday night!" This was always true of the original group, but honesty pulled through every girl that came to that living room. I finally figured it out:

My girlfriends are safe.

The room is void of all judgment, any criticism. Compassion is so thick you could pour it over pancakes. Lord knows there is nothing we won't say. We invite each other into our ugliest thoughts, our worst moments. No secret will ever be betrayed. No struggle is ever gossip fodder. We truly love each other. We're all a bucket of mess, so no one feels left out. It's like walking into a room with no walls.

Dear Ones, safe friends exist. They are a treasure that sometimes takes a little digging to find. The authors of *TrueFaced* explain the two extremes as living in the Room of Good Intentions and living in the Room of Grace. They say,

> I can't help but notice that in this room, The Room of Grace, everyone seems vitally alive. The people are obviously imperfect, full of compromise and struggle, but they're authentic enough to talk about it and ask for help. Many have a level of integrity, maturity, love, laughter, freedom, and vitality that I don't recall seeing in the people in the other room. I feel the start of something I haven't felt in . . . well, as long as I can remember. It's safety or something like it.[2]

Read Acts 9:20-22. This was immediately after Saul's conversion on the road to Damascus. (Need a refresher? Read 9:1-19.) Why couldn't the Jews accept him as a safe person?

There is a safety that exists only among believers. Not that non-Christians can't be good, even wonderful friends, but only believers can extend the grace they've experienced. A friend who belongs to Christ cares about you spiritually, and that alone will last. When you have to mask your faith or lessen its value, you're on dangerous ground.

What happens when you tell an unbelieving friend about the sacrifice God is calling you to? The ministry He's putting on your heart? The attitude He's lost patience for? There is no safety there because that perspective is foolishness to those who don't believe. None of us is perfect, but we must lock arms with girlfriends who can say, "We've both been lost, but we've both been found. Let's start from there."

Cloud and Townsend define safe people as those who do three things.[3] Let's learn them through the example of Barnabas, Son of Encouragement.

Trait #1: Safe people draw you closer to others.

Some girls just bring out the love in us, don't they? Their influence develops our compassion and helps us serve people better. Through their example, we learn to treat others with kindness. We discover mercy is more compelling than judgment. They don't entertain our gossip; they prefer our unity with other believers. My Girlfriend Leslie is like this. She listens to me like I'm the most fascinating girl on the planet, and she shares my feelings like they originated in her heart. I leave her thinking, *I'm going to be nice like Leslie today. I'll try for a whole hour.*

Read Acts 9:26-27. Why could Barnabas accept Saul when Jesus' other disciples could not? What was in his heart?

Barnabas was the bridge between Saul and Jesus' best friends, an alliance that changed the course of the church. This is our role as friends in Christ. Girls, if your friends reinforce divisions between you and other believers, danger! Our friends either nurture our bonds with others or they damage them, not only in the conversations they foster, but in *the way they are*. We need girlfriends who deepen our mercy for humanity rather than isolate us with gossip and contention.

A safe friend exhibits the following:

- She increases love within you.
- She makes you better in your other relationships.
- She counsels you toward forgiveness and reconciliation.
- She resists gossip.

- She loves other people well; she's not constantly at odds with others.
- She is confrontable, not defensive.
- You don't feel judged around her.
- She's not threatened by your other relationships.
- She's willing to say "I'm sorry" if necessary.
- She doesn't gripe about others constantly.

*Do your closest friends facilitate love or dissention between you and others? How?

Do you bring people together or reinforce their separateness?

Trait #2: Safe people help you become the woman God created you to be.

Don't you love a girlfriend who moves you closer to your purpose? The good ones say, "This is so your deal. I know you can do this." We have enough insecurities and fears to last us twenty lifetimes; we don't need friends who let us entertain them. Safe girlfriends help us become passionate wives, diligent moms, God's partners in ministry. They won't sit idly by while we waste away in sin. Their confrontations are wrought with love and absent of judgment. It's impossible to stay stagnant around them.

Read Acts 9:28-30. What might Saul's young ministry have looked like had Barnabas not created a safe place for him?

My Girlfriend Anna created a safe haven for the development of my writing ministry. Our dialogue went like this:
"I can't."

"Yes, you can. You're a good writer."

"No, I'm not. Plus I'm too young, scared, and obscure. And I've got a sassy mouth."

"Get started."

"I don't know how."

"I'll help you."

"I don't know where to go."

"I'll show you. We'll go together."

That girl wouldn't accept my best excuses. She was unwilling to let me shirk my calling. Yet her encouragement was godly, Spirit-led. I never felt bullied or coerced. Anna was simply committed to my purpose before I was. The day my first three books were released, she called and said, "Let's celebrate you." God's work is always a collaboration, even if one person gets the credit.

A safe friend exhibits the following:

- Her influence inspires you toward good works.
- She helps you become the woman God sees in you.
- She'll lovingly confront your issues—sin, fear, pride, whatever.
- You are a better person for knowing her.
- She is a growing believer.
- She encourages your development, but she loves you no matter how you are acting or what you are doing.
- She is not threatened by your successes.
- She is not disgusted by your failings.
- She is honest about her own shortcomings; there is no pride or self-sufficiency.

Do you have a friend committed to your healthy development? What does she do?

*Do you help your friends mature, or do you stunt their growth with negativity? What direction would they go if you were their only influence?

Trait #3: Safe people draw you closer to God.

This is distinct from helping us develop because some friends push us toward good works but not toward Christ. I have a friend involved in tons of ministry, but she recently told me, "I don't really know Jesus." I'd clearly spent way too much time talking shop with her and not nearly enough time talking about Jesus. The safest friend cares about your relationship with God more than any other facet of your life. Karla Worley wrote, "If we are faithful in this life, you will say of me and I will say of you, 'I knew Him better because I walked with her.'"[4]

Flip a few chapters to Acts 11:22-26. This was the first church made up of non-Jews. Barnabas was a *critical* New Testament player. What do you imagine this church looked like after a year with those two?

Aren't they wonderful? I can feel the enthusiasm leaping off this page in Acts. Girls, our inner circle must be women who adore God, because they'll help us love Him more. Safe friends nurture your relationship with Christ through their example, passion, and counsel. They'll ask the important questions: What are you learning? What is God doing in your life? They care about that. When we are angry or frustrated with God, they'll help bridge the gap. And we know it's not a sham because their relationship with God is as obvious as the effects of ultraviolet rays. They are wrinkles of godliness.

A safe friend exhibits the following:

- She consistently helps you become more like Christ.
- You learn who He is through her.
- She influences you toward time in the Word and in prayer.
- She asks what you're learning.
- She talks about what she's learning.
- She loves God; there's no mistaking it.
- You find yourself praying in new ways after being around her.
- She lovingly confronts your sin, and you don't feel judged.
- She's forgiving.
- She creates a hunger for God in you.
- You don't feel inferior around her.

*What is your experience with this kind of friend? Who has pushed you to Jesus? How?

How would your friends describe your relationship with God? How does it influence them?

Let it be said: Even the safest friends will have moments when they blow it; they are just people. We can never expect perfection from any friend. There is no girl who exhibits all these traits all the time. Safe people are mostly safe. This side of heaven, that's the best we can hope for. Don't review this day and decide there's no one *exactly* like this. Rather, discover that there are girls *a lot* like this.

I know it to be true. There are worthy friends out there for you, Believer. And don't mistake their "type" to be churchy, precious, and sugary. Safe friends can be sarcastic, hilarious, ornery, even downright stinkers. They will certainly have their own issues; safe friends are real girls. They'll struggle and fail sometimes. They might even let you down occasionally.

But at the end of the day, their friendship leads you from pretense to authenticity, from fear to laughter, from selfishness to godliness. They allow you to be on the outside who you are on the inside, and that's a gift. I beg you to receive it.

> Dear friends, let us love one another, for love comes from God. Everyone who loves has been born of God and knows God. (1 John 4:7)

Do you have safe friends? Thank God. Celebrate them. Do you need safe friends? Pray for them. Ask God to make you safe, as grace attracts grace.

What Not to Do

We'll spend the next two days on finding safe friends and evaluating the ones we have. We must begin the actual journey here because a good product is all about the right ingredients. It doesn't matter how much time you spent, how beautiful the frosting is, how splendid the serving piece; when you use baking soda instead of baking powder, your cake tastes like vomit (or so I've heard).

Choosing the right friends to speak into our lives will make or break the journey. As if I'm telling you something you don't know. None of us has gotten off scot-free relationally. This day is designed to spare you further injury and save you time. Girlfriends, Cloud and Townsend suggest there are poor strategies that don't work in finding safe people. They seem like excellent game plans, but they ultimately destroy our hope and cause conflict and isolation.[5]

Let Solomon, the wisest man on earth, teach you today.

Poor Strategy #1: Doing the Same Old Thing

You know the girl who has an angry and controlling dad, dates controlling boys, marries a controlling man, divorces him, marries another controlling man, and then cries to her counselor in despair? It's no secret that women repeat patterns. Duplicating sketchy history is a mistake many women make in friendship. We gravitate to certain types, even if they're toxic. Failure and pain don't teach us what God intended them to, and we play the same song over and over again.

 Read Proverbs 2:1-8. What are our responsibilities in gaining wisdom?

Cloud and Townsend observe, "When we don't sit back in an armchair with a cup of coffee after a failure and ask ourselves, 'Why?' we're likely to end up in the same place again."[6] Mistakes are inevitable, Dear Friends. Welcome to the human race. It's no indicator of wisdom to live a life absent of error. But the wise girl learns from those mistakes and alters her next course accordingly.

Review your history. Ask yourself the following questions:

- Do I have the exact same conversations with different women?
- Are my friendship problems similar (abandonment, control, guilt, gossip, irresponsibility)?
- Do my family and other friends see a pattern?
- Can I predict the end of a friendship?

*Are you drawn to unhealthy friends? Which kind?

If you had listened, what would God have taught you about your choices?

Poor Strategy #2: Doing the Opposite

Sometimes we make extreme moves on the heels of hurt. We decide that this type of girl is all bad, so the opposite type must be all good. And we leap out of the direct sunlight into the tanning bed. As an extremist, I have much empathy. It's easy to make a drastic decision after being injured.

If the girl who hurt me was irresponsible, my new best friend is the PTA president. If she subdued me with her mind control, I'll find a nice, passive doormat friend. I'll never befriend another impulsive girl again; if she's not severely predictable, she's off the candidate list. She's too liberal, so Condoleezza Rice, here I come. From chaotic to rigid, from judgmental to permissive, from party girl to Mother Teresa. We don't solve the problem. We just switch problems.

Read Proverbs 12:26. What is the difference between exercising caution in character discernment and reacting in an extreme manner?

Girls, there is beautiful wisdom in moderation. The worst girl has some redeeming qualities, and the best girl has a downside. Idealizing any one personality will disappoint you. Every friend must be cautiously evaluated, yes, but on her *wholeness*. Not on the one way she's the opposite from your last disastrous friendship, but how she is entirely. And even a failed relationship has one or two qualities you'd still like in the next. Caution doesn't throw every last similarity to the wind.

Girls, figure out the specific traits that wounded you rather than equating an entire personality with "good" or "bad." We're all a little of both. Crisscrossing across the landscape of friend-ship will wear you out and extinguish your hope.

 Have you made an extreme friend switch? What were you escaping or idealizing?

Poor Strategy #3: Doing Too Much

Often in the hunt for friends we throw ourselves into skill-based or functional activities: sports, book clubs, music groups, art classes, riding lessons, team moms, committees, school organizations. We're out there. We're rubbing elbows with other girls. We're talking about superficial details of life. And our hearts keep starving.

Or maybe we decide church is the place, so we join the mission team, the nursery committee, hospitality leadership, the office volunteer group. We're in there. We're planning important ministry. We're praying at the close of each meet-ing. And our hearts keep starving.

Read Ecclesiastes 4:7-10. This man spent all his time working and being productive but never connecting. "A miserable business" will mean *miserable busyness* if you're lonely. Why are work and activity inferior to meaningful relationships?

Girls, when we're in functional or task-oriented groups, relationships are more incidental than intentional. They can develop, but that's the exception. Connection is not the prior-ity; the activity is. Many women live here until the grave. They have much contact but no connection. They can list a hundred women who know their name but none who know their heart. There is no sharing of real self. John Powell wrote of this group dynamic, "Everyone remains safely in the isolation of his or her pretense, sham, sophistication. The whole group seems to gather in order to be lonely together."[7]

Have you forfeited deep friendship for superficial, activities-oriented acquaintances? What do you do?

*Do you intend to stay distant through fake community, or have you been confused by your loneliness?

Poor Strategy #4: Doing Nothing

This girl genuinely wants true friends, but she's doing nothing to make it happen. Perhaps bad friendships have scared her into paralysis. So she sits in silence, hoping that someone will come: "Please. Please." Or maybe a sketchy history has made her bitter: "*Of course* no one will come. Women are awful. See? My phone never rings." Sometimes a sense of entitlement keeps us sidelined: "If they want me, they'll ask me. I shouldn't have to drum up my own friends." Regardless, we sit on our haunches wondering why we're lonely week after week, year after year.

Read Proverbs 11:24-25. How do these verses translate to friendship?

Girls, if your heart wishes for friendship yet you never reach out to other women, it might help to address your aversion to taking risks and taking action. Stop responding to the big part of you that says, "This will never work" and learn to listen to the small part that says, "Pick up the phone!" Whether fear or passivity is at the root, how many chances have passed you by? This is a costly omission, Dear Ones. We get one shot at this life. Community is worth the risk every day and twice on Sunday.

*Do you have a hard time initiating contact or propelling a friendship? Why?

If you've done nothing, what is it costing you? How do you feel today?

Poor Strategy #5: Doing Without

Oh, my new Girlfriends, this is the graveyard after false solutions failed to deliver companionship. This is the loss of hope the Enemy was gunning for. Cloud and Townsend explain that with no one to tell you otherwise, "The very isolation of the dilemma is a judgment on you. It judges you in several ways, telling you things like:

- You aren't meant for safe people.
- You don't qualify.
- You've been asking for too much.
- You can't get it right.
- You are too damaged to have relationships.
- You aren't spiritual enough."[8]

Sure, you can still put on a pretty smile and life seems fine to the observer, but you are alone. You won't make a big deal out of it. You'll probably hide behind work, kids, activities, and such. But the detached part of your soul will wither away and die quietly, leaving you aching and incomplete. At some point you'll cut yourself off from those feelings just to survive. You'll make peace with hopelessness.

*Read Proverbs 24:13-14. How does wisdom in friend-
ship hold the promise of hope for us? Why do those
two go together?

Hope is Jesus' specialty. And lucky for us, so is wisdom.
He brings those two qualities together and stuns us with the
joys of godly, safe women who love us unconditionally. Your
aloneness grieves Him, Precious Friend. He has a better way.
When we add wisdom to friendship, there is hope, a hope of
communion and love, laughter and joy, understanding and
compassion.

We've all made mistakes. We've chosen poorly, acted irra-
tionally. We've entrusted ourselves to dangerous people and
suffered for it. We've sidelined wisdom for what seemed
better at the moment. Relationships have imploded, so we've
adopted some inferior strategies for next time. It's okay. We've
all done it.

But now we'll turn our ears to wisdom and apply our
hearts to understanding. We'll call out for insight and cry aloud
for discernment. We'll look for it as silver and search for it as
hidden treasure—we're ready for it. Then we'll understand
the fear of the Lord and find the knowledge of God. For the
Lord gives wisdom, and from his mouth come knowledge and
understanding. He holds victory in store for us—thank You,
Lord. He is our shield. He will guard our course and protect
the ways of His faithful ones. He is a God of safety.

Let's move forward, Faithful Ones.

Have poor strategies left you despairing? Pray for
discernment. Ask the Spirit to show you what is not
working. Cry aloud for understanding.

This Is the Beginning of a Beautiful Friendship

We lived for two years in Corpus Christi, a place I had to find on a map prior to moving. My husband joined a church staff there not knowing a soul. Our first baby was eight months old, I had to quit my job midway through the school year, and we were poor as paupers. Yeah, ministry!

Within two weeks we were invited to dinner at Tray and Jenny Pruet's, whoever they were. They earned immediate points for cooking fajitas. Their points doubled when they suggested Spades—girls versus boys, of course. They were pretty raunchy and fairly inappropriate, so I obviously thought this could go somewhere.

During cards, Jenny was eyeballing me across the table and struck up this conversation (and I quote it verbatim):

"Have you had a nose job?"

"No."

"Lip implants?"

"No."

"I just ask questions as they pop into my head."

"I like you."

And thus began a friendship to rival all friendships. We're on year eight together, though in separate cities now. We're getting ready for a cruise for their fortieth birthdays (they are my elders). Brandon and I define friendship through the love and laughter we've shared with the Pruets. We have since been unwilling to settle for anything less. And it all began over fajitas.

Discovering new friends is a lot like the early stages of dating. It's exciting. You're thrilled about the chemistry between you. Time together is fun and funny. But more than anything, you experience the bonds of connection you were created for. Stepping into God's vision always feels right.

I love everything written by John because he had such a tender heart. After all, he was the "disciple whom Jesus loved" (John 13:23). Those who've been loved well love well. He constantly called his readers "dear friends" and "my children." His tone was always endearing, adoring. And we're so lucky because he gave us a whole letter about discovering friendship. John teaches us the treasure of hospitality. It's how all friends get started.

He likely wrote 3 John while in his eighties. Tradition holds that John was working from Ephesus, the intellectual center of Asia Minor. John carried out an extensive evangelistic program from there, overseeing many of the churches he had founded and conducting a broad writing ministry. As the last living apostle, John was highly respected, and his testimony was authority.[9] Retirement, my eye.

The early church had come under attack by false teachers who were promoting Gnosticism (we'll save that for another study) and rejecting the teachers of the true gospel. John realized that the purity of the church must be protected in its infancy. And one way to save it was through hospitality.

Read 3 John 1-4. John mentioned Gaius's love for the truth three times in the first four verses. How important is it to you to identify "dear friend" candidates based on their love for God's truth? Your current friendships will indicate your priority.

This is challenging because church attendance doesn't qualify us by itself. We often believe that if we meet in the church lobby, friendship is automatically safe. And to be sure, looking for dear friends at church is certainly where I'd start. That's an excellent strategy, but the church is not a totally safe place, and it does not consist only of safe people.

With church people, we often think, *Since I found you at church, you should be good and trustworthy. Be kind to me. Protect me. Love me. You must be safe.* And so often they are, Girls. But we still must exercise discernment.

Thankfully, God allows unsafe people into His church. Otherwise I couldn't come. Neither could you. But He can make us safer. His church has been His hands and feet more times than we could count. The church can be a safety net, Friends. And those who really love the truth will be found in their Father's house.

Begin there.

Gaius, John's friend, was well-known for his safety. He loved new believers in his church and extended community to those traveling through. His kind reputation preceded him.

Read 3 John 5-8. What do you gather about Gaius in these verses?

Let's notice something about this dear friend: He reached out to strangers. If that puts a pit in your stomach, stay with me. They didn't begin by taking vacations together; it started in the comfort of Gaius's home. Girlfriends, this is where hospitality begins: "Come on over. Let's have a little coffee. I want to know you."

The best of friends, the most inseparable women on the planet, were once strangers. At some point, one of them reached out to the other. The earth didn't shake, the stars didn't fall from the sky, but a little spark flew. One offered a warm space; the other felt welcomed. And there began the dance of friendship.

Girls, God can use your hospitality to cultivate lifelong relationships. Just take a little leap. A simple invite. Mercifully, you don't need to entertain anyone. If that were the case, I'd have no friends. Forget putting on a show. Forget impressing her with your spotless house or perfect quiche. If you're looking for applause, this relationship is going nowhere. Just put on some coffee and give her the good chair. Shoes are optional.

In fact, John urged us to offer hospitality "in a manner worthy of God" (verse 6). God is not worried about impressing us or soliciting our approval. Nor does He put forward one side of Himself while withholding the real side. He values compassion and kindness. You know He loves to laugh. From first touch, God says, "This is who I am." He doesn't pursue us for what He can get but so that He can become our dear Friend.

*How do you feel about making the first move toward a "dear friend" candidate? Why do you answer like that?

List everything you see in verses 5-8 that qualify these believers as worthy of Gaius's hospitality.

These men were traveling missionaries, but my heart burns

to know they received "no help from the pagans" (verse 7). Girls, this unbelieving world is no help to God's children. They despise our faith, criticize our choices, ridicule our intelligence. It makes for awkward work environments and strained discussions. The Christian woman swims upstream, with the tidal waves of culture against her.

We can't leave each other to swim alone.

Most of us aren't missionaries, but don't we often feel like weary travelers through this life? Offering space to allow another believer to be known is to take part in Christ's ministry of togetherness. It may begin small as all friendships do, but in God's hands, it can transform into something wonderful, something supernatural, something that nourishes the deepest places of our spirit.

God creates dear friends.

We will talk face to face. Peace to you. The friends here send their greetings. Greet the friends there by name. (3 John 14)

Do you need to offer your hospitality — or your fears about it — to God? Pray for a name, a worthy "dear friend" candidate. Welcome her in. Pray for God's blessing.

Dig In: Betrayed

Maybe you're blessed in that you've been unscathed by a damaging friendship. You've known only safe friends who've loved you and made you better. But the majority can't say that. Most of us have been injured by a friend who was supposed to be on our side. It may have been last month; it might have been twenty years ago. But pain doesn't have an expiration date. Unaddressed, all it does is deepen and spread like cancer.

To that end, let's work with the Spirit on the most painful injury—that from a friend. It's hard to embrace godly friendships when you have a gaping wound. Before you begin, please pray. Ask the Spirit to soften your heart and create some space to move in you. If you've been hurt, start with an honest conversation with God about how you feel. No point in pretending.

In the later part of his reign (roughly 980 BC), David was threatened by a conspiracy under the leadership of his son Absalom, and his heart was broken. Absalom wanted the throne of Israel, and he instigated a rebellion against his own father to get it.

Adding insult to injury, Absalom sent for Ahithophel, David's closest counselor, to join the conspiracy. From then on, Ahithophel advised Absalom on conquering David, once his dear friend. The betrayal was multilayered involving his son, his friend, and his people, and David's grief was intense (2 Samuel 15–19). Many scholars believe he wrote Psalm 55 during this time.

Whether you've severed a relationship with a friend who betrayed you or you currently have a friend who hurts you, read David's words today with a heart that would prefer healing over retaliation. Work through the questions the Spirit leads you to in your journal.

Read 2 Samuel 15:5-12. Then read Psalm 55:1-3.

- In his heartbrokenness, David turned to God: "Hear me and answer me" (Psalm 55:2). What other avenues have you tried in light of a betrayal? Anger? Retaliation? Have you invited God in to do His thing?
- David's thoughts troubled him. What thoughts were running through his mind? Have you ever felt like he did? Do your thoughts and memories torture you?
- Absalom and Ahithophel truly brought emotional suffering on David. Friend, are you suffering like this? Was it someone else's anger that started this? Jealousy? What was the root of it?

Read 2 Samuel 15:13-18,30-31. Then read Psalm 55:4-11.

- David made Jerusalem his national capital (it had been Hebron previously), yet this betrayal forced him to flee to spare Jerusalem a bloodbath. Has a friend's betrayal forced you to leave your own place? Maybe your group of friends? Your church? Why did you leave?
- David wanted the wings of a dove so he could fly far

away to a place of shelter. Where is that for you? Did you find a safe place? Or did you stay in the war zone? What would the Spirit have you do? Ask Him.

- In both passages, David prayed that God would turn Ahithophel's counsel into foolishness. Friend, have you prayed for truth to prevail? God is on the side of right. Look deep. Have you saddled your feelings to anything false? Is your version a twist of truth at all? Pray for you and your friend to become covered in rightness.

Read 2 Samuel 16:5-12. Then read Psalm 55:12-14.

- This betrayal left David so devastated that he couldn't find the strength to ward off curses from Shimei, a member of Saul's family from whom David took the throne. What emotions do you see in David in this passage? Are you beaten down, too? Have you allowed someone to kick you while you were down? Who?
- David spoke of the worst kind of betrayal: "My son, who is of my own flesh, is trying to take my life" (2 Samuel 16:11). Friend, is your pain increased because of who wounded you? What did your relationship used to look like?
- Will you identify with Jesus? Will you go with Him when He was betrayed by Judas? Denied by Peter? Crucified by the people He came to save? Ask Him to minister to you. No one understands better.

Read Psalm 55:16-22.

- There is no place your pain should take you than to God's own throne. Bitterness, anger, hurt feelings will never heal you, Friend. Cry out to Him. Let Him shoulder your distress. Say every word you need to say.

- Verse 18 in the NASB says, "He will redeem my soul *in peace* from the battle which is against me." Do you believe this? Do you know that God can render you unharmed? He can rescue you, but you must stop trying to rescue yourself. Ask Him what you need to let go of.
- If your betrayer never changes his or her ways, God can still heal you. This person does not have to be sorry in order for God to move. Is this what holds you back? Will you ask God to help you release that need? If your betrayer's lack of remorse keeps you paralyzed, he or she is still controlling you.
- Please hear this: God will never let the righteous fall. Check His history. Ask Him to show you any action or attitude that keeps you from righteousness. Help Him work redemption in your life.

Oh, I love you, Friend. The human experience can be so painful, but "we do not have a high priest who is unable to sympathize with our weaknesses" (Hebrews 4:15). Jesus knows how you feel. He also knows there is life on the other side. He is the Savior of reconciliation. His Father is the Healer. The Spirit leads us. There is no break too difficult for those three to handle.

If you've been devastated by the wounds of a friend, I pray you would choose to be healed. God can and would do that for you. You alone keep yourself rooted in pain. If you'll bravely offer God your forgiveness, He can turn that sacrifice into radical wholeness. I can't explain it. It's supernatural. Our instincts tell us to hold on to anger; it seems like self-preservation. Forgiveness leads to vulnerability, which feels too risky after a betrayal. But your forgiveness does not open you back up to injury. It frees you up for joy again. It allows you to release the hurt and bitterness; they are so heavy to carry.

If nothing else, do you want to feel this pain forever? Is this working for you? Our dear Jesus said, "*Friend*, your sins are forgiven" (Luke 5:20). Indeed, He forgave Peter, the Jews, the sins of the whole world. It's the better way. I pray you are able to believe Him.

> Cast your cares on the LORD
>> and he will sustain you;
>> he will never let the righteous fall.
>>> (Psalm 55:22)

WEEK FOUR

The Gift of Gab

Opening Up

I remember a conversation I had with my Girlfriend April when we were first getting to know each other. We'd advanced past "Where did you grow up?" and "What do you do?" I'd seen sarcasm in her that held the promise of connection for us, so I cautiously tested the real waters with her:

"Do you ever lose your patience with your kids?" I asked carefully.

"Maybe. Do you?"

"Sometimes I lock myself in my room and pretend I can't hear them."

"Sometimes I lock them in the backyard and pretend I can't hear them knocking."

"I accidentally told my kids we had children so they could be our slaves," I confessed.

"I once asked my mother-in-law if she'd apply to be their foster mother."

"I watch *American Idol*."

"I've never missed an episode of *The Bachelor*."

"Let's be friends."

In their book *I Know Just What You Mean*, Ellen Goodman and Patricia O'Brien wrote, "Talk is at the very heart of women's friendships, the core of the way women connect. It's the given, the absolute assumption of friendship . . . a living current of conversation. . . . In these ongoing dialogues, women reveal themselves. Gradually, trust is tested and won; an intimate comfort zone is created."[1]

This is how women begin the waltz of friendship. Talking is not inconsequential. It is serious business in the community of women. While men connect by doing, women connect by talking. To share the details of our lives is to hold out the offer of companionship. It is the beginning point of something more. It's where we discover commonalities, empathy, shared experiences. Talk is the breeding ground of intimacy.

Girls, we have much to learn from Paul. His letters are so full of affection that we simply must read closer and find out why. Where did it come from? How did Paul act with his new friends to form such tight bonds? If we pay attention, we'll learn some excellent tips on talking that leads to community.

Read 1 Thessalonians 2:1-3. What must have happened to Paul and his friends in Philippi?

Can you pick up on how it made Paul feel?

Luke tells us a few things they endured in Philippi: false accusations, public stripping and beating, flogging, imprisonment, torture, injustice, rejection (Acts 16:11-40). It wasn't a pleasant stay. When Paul briefly mentions their suffering, he's playing it way down. A normal person would never recover from their experience. Trauma and fear would suffocate any similar exposure later. At best, we'd hope to see some private healing under the cover of obscurity until death swept in and silenced the bad memories.

But Paul walked straight to Thessalonica, still bearing the stripes of his torture. He opened his heart up to the Thessalonians just as he had to the Philippians. Fear did not lock him out of future relationships. "With the help of our God" he moved forward (1 Thessalonians 2:2). He dared to open his mouth once again.

Friend, regardless of your history, with God's help you can open up to another woman again. It won't eliminate any pain you've incurred, any betrayal, any disclosure of something you shared in confidence. It won't erase your wounds or bless you with amnesia. But it is the avenue to healing. Only in personal connections can God use the "cords of human kindness" (Hosea 11:4), one of His best tools. By holding back because of history, you miss the treasure of future friends.

 Has opening up to another woman ever come back to hurt you? What happened?

Let's learn about this opening-up process from Paul. If anyone knew the importance of exercising discernment in this area, he did. He knew the sting of betrayal, but he also experienced the joy of fellowship. We can be sure that every time he opened his mouth to speak, he weighed his words carefully.

Read 1 Thessalonians 2:4-6. When women open up by talking, in what ways do we:

- try to please women instead of God?
- use flattery?
- put on masks to cover up?
- look for praise from women?

Wouldn't you think Paul would be tempted to use those tactics? Transparency netted him a vicious flogging. At least he could have taken a subtle approach in Thessalonica, maybe a soft-sell style. Perhaps a teeny bit of flattery would've worked better. Didn't he want to protect his life? His heart?

Girls, Paul understood that those self-protective methods do nothing of the sort. They don't deliver what they promise. So he and his friends came in with pure motives, soft hearts toward God's purposes. They wouldn't try to cushion their communication or insulate the truth. They came to the Thessalonians honestly, openly, willing to go to the deep with them, too.

*Of the tactics previously listed, which talking tool do you use with other women most? Why?

In *Why Am I Afraid to Tell You Who I Am?*, John Powell discussed five levels of communication, ranging from the most guarded to total relational freedom:[2]

1. Level Five: Cliché Conversation
   This is the conversation of the cocktail party, the club meeting, the church lobby: "How are you? How're the kids? I like your shoes. Good to see you. Fine, thanks. Just great." There is absolutely no sharing of real self. We mean almost nothing of what we're saying or asking. It's obligatory, polite chitchat, void of true connection.
2. Level Four: Reporting the Facts About Others
   This is a small step forward, but we still expose almost nothing of ourselves. We talk about what she did and what they're planning. Communication is formed around little gossip items and conversation pieces. It's not about me or you, but them or that. Neither is it our emotions on the subject, but rather just the facts.

3. Level Three: My Ideas and Judgments

   This is the first time we step cautiously out. I'll tell
   you my conclusions on stuff. We don't yet attach our
   deep feelings to our ideas, but we trot them out for a
   test run: "I like this. I don't like that. I've decided to try
   this out. I think this about that." Level Three is dicey
   though; we are watching the other person closely. If
   she seems irritated (bored, skeptical, confused, shocked,
   uninterested), we're out of there. We'll either shut
   down or start saying things to please her.

4. Level Two: My Feelings (Emotions) "Gut Level"

   This level is our goal. Surprisingly, there is much more
   to share after our ideas are broadcasted. It is our feelings
   about those things that truly communicate who we
   are. Our ideas are pretty standard, actually, but our
   feelings that lie under those judgments are uniquely
   ours. And it is here that we progress to the deep end.
   For example, in the chart that follows, an idea is listed
   on the left, but some possible corresponding emotions
   are on the right:

I think you're a   . . . and I'm jealous.
great mom . . .

                        . . . and I feel insecure
                            around you.

                        . . . and I really admire you.

                        . . . and I kind of want to
                            compete with you.

                        . . . and I'm always trying to
                            sell myself to you.

                        . . . and it gives me a lot of
                            hope.

Most of us feel as though other women couldn't handle this level of honesty, so we never go this far. The true stuff remains buried, and the relationship stays superficial. This gut-level communication is where it gets real.

5. Level One: Peak Communication

This is one step beyond gut-level communication and is not a permanent experience. This is the connection that happens between two people when they share a moment so perfectly, it's as if the same emotion registers in two hearts. This often happens in crisis or victory. Each woman knows that her reactions are shared completely by her friend. It is a friendship moment that occurs between two girls committed to gut-level talking. Their relationship is prepared for this level of intimacy.

Do you tend to get stuck in a lower level of communication? Which one? Why?

*Do you share gut-level communication with any friend? If so, what is it like? If not, what keeps you from this kind of honesty?

Does anyone share gut-level communication with you? If so, how do you respond? If not, how would you respond?

Girls, safe friends can handle this. They respect your emotions. They love your feelings because they love you. Believe me, there are women who will not be shocked by your selfishness. You can tell them. You can describe your fears and insecurities. They'll stick around. They are safe receivers of your dreams and desires. They'll guard the deepest places of you. These friends will listen to your feelings about them, even if they're hard to say. Try this out on a safe friend. You'll see.

Talking is how our friends know us, and in it, we come to know ourselves. Karla Worley wrote, "'Know me' is the cry of a woman's heart."[3] It is here we journey on together. In sharing the truth, we move closer to God's holiness. He is a friend of truth, remember. Our deepest feelings are brought into the light where, together, we are able to evaluate the direction they are taking us.

*Read 1 Thessalonians 2:7-8. What was Paul saying about opening up?

There is a point, Dear Girlfriends, when we move from sharing the facts to sharing our lives. After safety is established and trust is earned, it is delightful to invite a friend into the knowledge of you. Paul was right. It is from this place that we truly begin growing in the body of Christ, as Jesus wanted us to all along. We discover that our honesty is not a burden on each other, but a treasure. There is nothing more valuable you can offer your friend than yourself.

Give it away.

Be honest with the Spirit about what you think about gut-level communication — giving it and receiving it. Tell Him your concerns, but also ask for His insight. Ask Him what your next step should be.

Permission To Speak Honestly

Last night at Bible study our Girlfriend Denise was telling us about a problem with a friend. Denise came to Christ last year, and her life completely changed. She was in a toxic marriage years ago that ended in divorce but produced two dear sons. She later married a wonderful man, and they've blended their families beautifully. Her oldest son is not a believer, but Denise loves him gently and lives Jesus clearly. We've all commissioned him to the Holy Spirit.

Her friend, who has been in her life for twenty years, repeatedly tells Denise what a poor job she did with her oldest son. She condemns her lifestyle during those years and points to her son's life as evidence. She heaps guilt on Denise in nearly every conversation.

As she told us this, our mouths dropped.

"What?! What do you say to her?" I screeched.

"Nothing. I just listen."

I launched into a rant on healthy relationships and the value of honest confrontations. I did a little preachin' on redemption, too. (It might not surprise you to know that I sometimes get a little worked up.) When I finally came up for air, I asked

Denise, who I'd pushed to tears by now, "How long has this been going on?"

"Seven years."

"Denise. Please tell me you're joking."

"I just don't want to damage our friendship by saying something."

Lord, have mercy.

Girlfriends, I know some of you struggled yesterday with gut-level communication, that honest presentation of self that attaches our feelings to our ideas. It refuses to leave our emotions buried in repression and chooses to present them instead. And as you read that, you thought, *Well, this has been fun. Good-bye, everyone!*

Quite frankly, we're not willing to tell this kind of truth because of the tension we think it will bring into our relationships. We assume it will not be received well, so we hide it. We make a calculated decision not to speak openly because we attach a higher value on keeping the peace than on authenticity. I bet nearly every one of us is in a relationship with someone—a husband, son, daughter, friend, coworker, boss, neighbor, sister—who has no idea we are covering up our true feelings about him or her or something he or she does.

Do you have a friend who is unaware of your inner struggle with her?

In *The Real Deal*, Bill Hybels calls these pseudocommunal relationships. He wrote, "[These relationships] are those that have the pretense and appearance of community, but in which real community doesn't exist. We sacrifice truth-telling on the altar of peacekeeping and never enter into real community."[4] A thousand "what ifs" haunt us: What if she gets mad? What if she's crushed? What if she doesn't understand? What if our friendship is ruined? What if everything changes?

Once again, God is on the side of truth. Withholding truth out of fear is not godly, Friend. If He is indeed for truth, then He will also defend it, protect it, use it, and bless it. That is the truth. The Enemy whispers those "what ifs" to keep us from real union. But God unites us through honesty. It is a tool for intimacy, a catalyst for spiritual growth. He's told us that only ten thousand times in His Word.

I know. It's just that we treasure our girlfriends, and we don't want to hurt those relationships. We love them, even if their behavior is painful or destructive in this or that area. Let me show you something in Scripture today. Remember that Paul came to Christ after the Resurrection. He was welcomed and equipped through Jesus' disciples, thanks to Barnabas. James, Peter, John — they were his first mentors.

Read Galatians 2:7-10. In Paul's description of his early ministry to the Galatians, what dynamic do you pick up on between him and Peter?

Peter, James, and John were mentors, co-laborers in the gospel, truly pillars of this young faith in Jesus. Theirs were household names among the early church. Peter took Paul in for two weeks at one point after his conversion (Galatians 1:18). They were brothers in Christ, one teaching and stretching the other. I can imagine Paul sitting in Peter's living room begging for more details: "What was He like? Tell me everything."

But even the dearest relationships can hit a snag. No one is above temptation or struggle, nor should we expect anyone to be. See, there was a group of Jews who were adamant that Gentiles must be circumcised according to Jewish custom once they became believers. For them, keeping the Jewish law was the absolute necessary response to salvation. The Gentiles' neglect of this custom was too offensive for them to overcome, and they began teaching that pleasing God was conditional upon circumcision.

It was driving a dangerous wedge between Jewish and non-Jewish believers.

*Is there something (an attitude, a discussion, a habit, an issue) that is driving an internal wedge between you and a friend? What is it, even if she doesn't know?

The danger with this is assuming that if you don't address it, it will go away. Listen to this:

> If I tell you that it bothers me when you do something you are accustomed to doing, I may be tempted to believe that it would be better not to mention it. Our relationship will be more peaceful. You wouldn't understand, anyway. So I keep it inside myself, and each time you do your thing my stomach keeps score—2 . . . 3 . . . 4 . . . 5 . . . 6 . . . 7 . . . 8. . . . Then one day you do the same thing that you have always done and all hell breaks loose. All the while I was feeling annoyed, I was keeping it inside and somewhere, secretly, learning to hate you.[5]

Welcome to Satan's secret.

He knows our omissions are not neutral. They are altogether harmful. They slowly turn our love for each other into gall. They build rather than dissipate until they erupt in a violent display, truly ruining the relationship, or they suffocate what was lovely between us until it withers and dies. It's a private assault on unity, and before the other person knows it even exists, it is too late.

If you identified an unspoken issue between you and a friend, how are you beginning to feel about her? Act toward her? Be honest.

I'm sure Paul dealt with similar feelings toward Peter. See, I adore Peter, but he got wrapped up in this circumcision-after-salvation thing. It happened to be the Jewish leaders making the fuss, and Peter didn't want to rock the boat. He didn't jump on their bandwagon entirely, but he started treating the Gentiles differently. All of a sudden there was a lot less grace and a lot more judgment. And Paul heard about it.

Read Galatians 2:11-16. Yikes. What are some worries that might have plagued Paul before this confrontation?

*What worries you about speaking the truth to your friend?

I must ask you: Is your relationship as it is now working for you? Is your silence worth your heartache? Could speaking honestly be any worse than how you're feeling privately? And since I'm going there, are you doing your friend a favor by ignoring the problem? Is this helping her grow? Is it using your love to bring both of you closer to Jesus? Is it making your friendship stronger?

This is why truth wins: It leads us to maturity. It is entirely possible to speak truthfully and maintain love. You can say, "I love you and value you more than I can express, so this is hard for me to say. I don't want this conversation to upset you, and the last thing I'm trying to do is sting you. But I need to tell you how I'm feeling. This may be as hard to hear as it is to say, but I'm willing to go through the chaos for the sake of our relationship. I care about you and us too much to let this fester any longer. I'm going to be honest, and I want you to feel the freedom to be honest with me, too."

Remember how Jesus came to us: full of truth and grace.

How did it work out between Peter and Paul? This issue threatened to split the early church, so a meeting was called in Jerusalem to address it once and for all. Could Gentiles possibly please God without being circumcised? The apostles, Peter and Barnabas, and the elders all converged, but not before Paul had some time with Peter. We read their confrontation in Galatians, but Luke shares the fruits of it in Acts.

*Read Acts 15:6-12. How did the Holy Spirit use this honest confrontation for His purposes?

Satan is a liar. It is *not* better to stay silent and let sin and hurt wreck a friendship. Together, Peter and Paul addressed the council, and the early church was saved from extinction. It must have been hard for Paul to say those words to his friend, his mentor. But because God is on the side of right, their relationship was strengthened, not diminished. Peter didn't leave in a huff or instigate a faction against Paul. Through a friend's honesty, Peter was stretched toward maturity, and he stood boldly moments later, declaring the freedom of salvation for Gentiles.

Believer, God can perform the same miracle in your relationships. He not only can preserve your friendship, but He can also mature both of you and use you for His kingdom. You can do this. If you want anything beyond a pseudocommunity, you must do this. Make a deal with Him: You'll give God your fear, and He'll give you His favor.

Everyone wins.

Do you have a confrontation coming? Ask the Spirit for wisdom, discernment, and kindness. Pray for the chance to speak and the words to say.

The Sideways Approach

My Girlfriend Trina is the easiest person in the universe to read. She thinks she's being neutral, but I can spot her attitude in half a second. My Girlfriend Leslie and I laugh about this (to Trina's face) because we love her so much.

Trina does her body language thing mainly in church settings. The reason this is funny is because she is a pastor's wife. She came to Christ as an adult, so she never reconciled the weird way Christians behave when they're in a group together. I was formally trained in church-speak through Sunday school, GAs, VBS, children's choir, WMU, prayer meetings, church training, visitation, Christian concerts, Wednesday night dinners, Bible studies, youth group, church camp, mission trips, Easter cantatas, revivals, retreats, and conferences. Have mercy. It's a miracle I'm as normal as I am.

Where was I?

Oh, yes. Trina. Having no formal training in Christianese, she finds it odd how women talk and act more spiritual all of a sudden when they get together under the banner of some church thing. So she crosses her arms and fidgets with her fingers. It's an interesting fidget. Hand wringing, really. A few minutes later, one foot starts shaking like it's having a seizure. And when she really gets pushed, she sighs out loud, believing we can't hear it. So help me, it's true. A big, fat sigh.

At this point, I make eye contact with her to pass on a message: "Pull it together. You're at Level Three exasperation." This is never effective, though, because I'm too busy laughing. You'd have to be an idiot to miss her real feelings. Or be too preoccupied talking churchy talk to notice.

Like Trina, we also have alternatives to speaking honestly, Girls. Our feelings are too strong to completely conceal, so they come out in other ways. And as you can imagine, these ways are neither effective nor subtle. We avoid the dead dog and get hit by oncoming traffic instead. (Of course, *we* don't. Our friends do. Let's pray for them.)

How do your feelings generally slip out when you are unwilling to be direct about them?

Read Ephesians 4:20-24. As it applies to honest friendships, list everything you can think of that characterizes the "old self." How does the old self act with others?

What should change with the new self? How does this new self, *created to be like God*, act with others?

This really bugs me sometimes. Don't get me wrong: There's plenty I like about the new self. I'm a fan of forgiveness, redemption. But getting rid of that old self is an area I often wish God would keep His paws off. Why can't He just let us enjoy the new and keep the parts of the old that we still like?

The old self doesn't have to think about others. We don't have to care about their spiritual lives. In fact, my favorite part of the old self is her motto: It really is all about me. We can look out for number one every second of every day, and no one can tell us otherwise. If we don't feel like doing the work of a real relationship, we can simply leave it behind. Her loss. If I'm mad, I can just gossip. Yeah, gossip! Feels so good. Or if I'm of that persuasion, I'll just verbally slash her soul out and leave her for dead. Good-bye.

But Paul tells us, "Put off your old self, which is being corrupted by its deceitful desires" (verse 22).

*Read Ephesians 4:25-27. What do you think Paul knew about unresolved anger?

Yesterday we talked about the best way to deal with breaches in relationships. Just go there honestly, lovingly. Speak the truth because you love your friend and value her presence in your life. Today we'll look at four inferior alternatives and expose their harmfulness.[6] Rather than speak honestly, many of us adopt one of the following tactics.

Inferior Tactic #1: Hint Dropping

This girl wants reconciliation but tries to build it with carefully constructed suggestions and hints. She attempts to communicate her feelings without actually saying them. If she is feeling wronged, you'll never hear it directly. Rather, she'll drop subtle stabs into your conversation, referencing her feelings but never expressing them.

"I guess you'll be spending your weekend with Rachel . . . your new, fun friend."

"I'm thinking about taking you off my caller ID!"

"I love how Amy treats me. I never feel criticized by her!"

"I asked Stacy to help me because I can really count on her."

This is an immature approach to communication, one I've been guilty of. There is no ownership here, and hint dropping tends to hurt the recipient, who does indeed pick up on her subtlety. No healthy adult responds well to this kind of condescension.

Read Ephesians 4:29. How does hint dropping tear our friend down rather than build her up?

Inferior Tactic #2: Manipulating

This girl wants to address conflict, but she can't seem to be honest. Instead, she pressures and manipulates her friend into doing what she wants. She often sees the other person, not her communication, as the problem. When she encounters conflict, she twists it rather than confronting it.

"Everyone else sees it my way."
"That's just your insecurity talking."
"You really should do this. It's best for everyone."
"It's not Christlike to always think of yourself."

Rather than discussing issues honestly and owning her feelings, she projects her opinions through manipulation, playing on her friend's weaknesses. There is no attempt at mutuality, only control. Her friend ends up feeling bullied, and the friendship is lopsided.

Read Ephesians 4:30-31. Why do you think this kind of communication grieves the Holy Spirit? What is He grieving?

Inferior Tactic #3: Guilt Tripping

This girl might be truly hurt, but instead of being honest, she heaps a load of guilt onto her friend with her slicing commentary. She usually has a bit of a martyr syndrome and feels entitled to perfect behavior from her friends.

"After all I've done for you, this is how you treat me?"
"Don't worry about me. I'll handle this myself. I'm sure I'll be fine."
"No problem. I'll just find someone else who has time for me."
"I know you don't understand. Your life is perfect."

She is hoping that through her predicament, her neediness, or her pathetic presentation, she can guilt her friends into community. This is a childish way to communicate, and it will sustain a friendship for only a short while.

Read Ephesians 4:32. What does forgiving others as Christ forgave us look like?

Why is the guilt tripper so far off this mark?

Inferior Tactic #4: Stonewalling

This girl doesn't enjoy confrontation, but she can't hold her displeasure in either. So she pouts. She withdraws. She becomes the queen of the one-word answers. Her silence speaks loudly, and she uses it to punish the friend who hurt her.

"Are you okay?"

"Fine."

"Are you coming?"
"Whatever."

"Is something wrong?"
"No."

"Are you upset?"
"I said no!"

Meanwhile, you can cut the resentment with a knife. She wants you to know you hurt her, but she is reluctant to be honest about the details. The typical end to this relationship comes when her friend is no longer willing to endure her pouting and moves on.

Read Ephesians 4:25 again. If we are all members of one body, how does stonewalling ultimately hurt the person who is withdrawing?

*Okay, Dear Girlfriends, of the four inferior tactics we've discussed—hint dropping, manipulating, guilt tripping, and stonewalling—do you see any unhealthy communication patterns you've used instead of honesty? If so, which do you typically employ?

Would you be willing to ask forgiveness from your friend for these indirect approaches and then commit to gritty honesty?

It's so hilarious that we're willing to act ugly in these ways, but we're scared to tell the truth. It is far worse to communicate with backhanded comments and seething hostility than to simply say, "I'm feeling hurt by something you did. You probably didn't mean to at all, but this is how I felt."

We take these shortcuts because we're trying to keep the peace, but we end up sabotaging the very peace we wanted to protect. If I sound like a broken record, forgive me, but God does not lead us wrong, Believer. If He says, "Speak the truth," we should. If He says, "Forgive," we should. If He says, "Don't let the sun go down on your anger," we shouldn't. Not only because we want to be obedient but because *it is the better way*. We see fear and confrontation, but God sees restoration and maturity. We see possible alternatives to dealing with our feelings, but God sees a train wreck.

Will you try His way? The next time your feelings rise up with a friend—which is normal and fine—will you choose to deal with them honestly? Recognize your temptation to skirt the issue, take a deep breath, and say, "I've got to be honest with you. That made me feel bad." If you're dealing with a safe friend, she'll look you in the eye and say, "I'm sorry. Let's set this right."

And together you'll put a little more grace into the world.

Will you let the Spirit search the ways you communicate? If necessary, will you repent of the false ways you've dealt with your friends? God loves real relationships.

Dirty Mouth? Clean It Up!

There are some stereotypes about women that irritate me. For instance, we are not all ignorant when it comes to sports. In fact, I love college football so much that we literally schedule our life around games. I can talk to a man about a safety, clip, touchback, audible, illegal block, screen pass, and interference. I know who the first-round draft picks were. I know what the preseason polls say. I know which matchups are on ESPN College GameDay. The burnt orange section of my closet gets regular wear.

I really want you to like me, and I hope I didn't just mess that up. I still love high heels. I'm a fan of highlights and pedicures. I like cute clothes and such. It's just that if you call me during the game, I'll screen you like you're a representative from my Visa account. It's one of those ways I'm not very girly in the traditional sense.

Having said that, there is a stereotype about women that I hate more than any of them, primarily because it's true. I'll give you some hints: It has to do with our mouths. It usually involves other people. Those people are never there to defend themselves. It is mean. It gets nasty. It can set off a frenzy of similar behavior until we feel like we need a shower.

Ugly talk.

Heaven help us, women can slice and dice with our words, can't we? While men are rather clumsy in this area, women can zero in on someone's weakest spot like a tractor beam. Because we are more perceptive, more sensitive, we can inflict greater damage with our words. And sometimes we're just mean and like to talk about other people. True?

In conversations with your friends, if 1 is entirely positive talk and 10 is entirely negative talk, where do you fall? Where do your closest friends fall?

Dearest Girlfriends, we must rise up together and change this. We simply must. As believers, we cannot carry on with gossip, slander, and negativity anymore. While we must journey together, and talking is our footpath, what we say will either display or destroy the unity God intended. Let's pick up where we left off yesterday in Ephesians and see if Paul can help us.

Let's start with Ephesians 5:1-2. Land sakes! What should the life of a believer look like? List everything you see in these two verses.

Have you ever read two verses packed with more punch? Frankly, when I hear that I should act just like Jesus did, I go to the fetal position. *Just like Him?* That selflessness? Those sacrifices? That compassion? His aching love for other people? A fragrant offering? This one directive should inform every word that seeps from our mouths, every manner in which we encounter other people.

Because we are so dearly loved, Friends, we should live a life of love. Henri Nouwen wrote, "It is remarkable how easy it is to bless others, to speak good things to and about them, to call forth their beauty and truth, when you yourself are in touch with your own blessedness. The blessed one always blesses."[7]

Women who have allowed God to love them lavishly naturally pour it back out. They are less likely to engage in destructive conversations because their hearts are full of gratefulness. They stand in grace, adored. They know it. They choose to believe God when He says, "My unfailing love for you will not be shaken" (Isaiah 54:10). Well then, my stars. Let a new life of love begin. What else is there to do?

*Do you see a correlation between how you talk (to and about others) and how you've received God's unfailing love? What link do you see?

"Live a life of love." Hmm. This is something we say a lot in church circles, but what does that look like? A life of love loves everyone else, even our nonfavorites. A life of love is concerned with building our husbands up, not tearing them down to our friends. This life wants to love other women, both to their faces and behind their backs. At any given moment, I can ask myself, "Am I living a life of love?" and very often, the answer is not good.

A life of love isn't one good moment of love. I've got plenty of moments when I think, *I am being such a good person.* But do those moments characterize my life, or do they stand as exceptions? If they're just for show, then they don't count. If every word out of my mouth was weighed over the course of a day, a month, what would the verdict be? Jen lives a life of _____. Sarcasm? Contradictions? Negativity? Selfishness? Judgment?

I'm just saying.

Read Ephesians 5:3-4. Not even a hint? Gracious. Girls, think about your conversations with other women. When have you talked about a hint, if not more, of any of the following?

- Sexual immorality
- Any kind of impurity (including gossip)
- Greed (the longing for more stuff than you already have)
- Obscenity
- Foolish talk (such as how fat you feel or how fat somebody else is or obsessing in other ways that don't feed anybody's soul)
- Coarse joking (including jabs at other people)

*Which of these are hardest for you to avoid? Why do you suppose that's the case?

Is there any chance you use your faith to justify it or spin it? How?

Paul was writing to a church and warned of these talking patterns "among you" (verse 3). I don't mean to shock you, but Christian women can have nasty mouths. What?! No! Yes, Sweet Little Lambs, it's true. Of course, you and your friends don't struggle here, but others do.

And isn't it lovely how Christians repackage gossip as prayer requests? "I'm really concerned about her. I'm not spreading rumors; I'm worried." Friends, garbage by any other name still stinks. No matter what churchy spin we put on gossip, God is not fooled. Nor would that friend be—or your husband, if he's the target—if she heard you broadcasting her business.

We cannot run our mouths unchecked under the banner of righteousness.

God won't stand for it. Listen to what He says:

"I am against the prophets who steal from one another words supposedly from me. Yes," declares the LORD, "I am against the prophets who wag their own tongues and yet declare, 'The LORD declares.' Indeed, I am against those who prophesy false dreams," declares the LORD. "They tell them and lead my people astray with their reckless lies, yet I did not send or appoint them. They do not benefit these people in the least," declares the LORD. (Jeremiah 23:30-32)

Check the general tone of your conversations with girlfriends. What do you talk about? Other girls? Your weekly gripes about your husband? Complaints about your church? Everything that's wrong with your life? How you're such a saint for enduring the life your family is handing you? How screwed up everyone else is? Badness? Sadness? Madness?

Girls, it is far superior to "not let any unwholesome talk come out of your mouths, but only what is helpful for building others up according to their needs, that it may benefit those who listen" (Ephesians 4:29). It just is. How much better do you feel off the heels of an encouraging conversation rather than one stinging with bitterness? Those toxic discussions are like a torrential river, slowly eroding away your gentleness, your optimism.

Gossip is so tempting because you and I get to share it. Together, we know something. We can carry on a private commentary on it. Dear One, the next time a piece of information burns to be shared about someone else, don't say it. Please don't. Ask the Holy Spirit to immediately exchange that thought for a unity-friendly one.

Find something else to share with that girlfriend *that minute*.

What can you tell her about you? Your spiritual walk? Something you want to try? Your most pressing issue? How can she pray for you? How can she counsel you? Talk about something you've been pondering. Share an inner struggle you've been unwilling to discuss. Laugh. Be kind. Be silly instead. Tell her the best thing that happened to you that week. Talk about what God is teaching you, where He's leading you.

Or what can you say instead that would encourage your friend? What blessings can you speak to her? What loveliness can you highlight in her? How can you support her? Point her to Christ? Carry a burden? Thank her for something she has done. Thank her for who she is. Tell her your favorite thing about her. Tell her what godliness you've seen in her lately.

What would your friendships look like if you replaced every negative comment with a gracious word instead?

Would any one relationship completely change? What does that tell you?

*Does avoiding negativity seem inconsistent with being honest and open? What's the difference between being honest and being toxic?

As girlfriends in Christ, let us talk like dearly loved children of God, a group of girls who found out they are God's favorites. He loves to see the kids getting along. Our capacity to build one another up is astonishing. Our words possess healing. Our conversations can mimic the dynamic between

Father and Son. God has truly given us the gift of influence over each other.

Let's wield it carefully.

Friend, ask the Spirit if your talk is pleasing Him or grieving Him. Search your friendships in this area. Ask to discover your own blessedness. It will change every word that comes out of your mouth.

Dig In: Hearing the Truth

*I*n good friendships, there comes a point when your dear friend, the one you love, the one who has been all over the map with you, needs to say some hard things to you. We do not relish these moments. We don't love being called out or challenged on bad behavior. Nor do we enjoy hearing that we hurt our friend, intentionally or not. It stinks to discover that someone else can see the trouble spot we thought we were hiding so well.

But if she loves you, if she loves the truth and all the goodness that comes with it, then she will be unwilling to let an issue hurt you or divide your friendship. This is the mark of a mature friend, and you are lucky to have her. Superficial friends always prefer your comfort over your godliness. But know this: They may protect your comfort in the short-term, but they do you no favors if you intend on growing beyond today. Nor will that friendship be given the opportunity to flourish as God intended it to.

That said, it's hard to hear the truth. Our human nature bucks that confrontation. Let's work through some wisdom from Solomon today that might help. If God is indeed on the side of truth, then we'd better learn how to receive it.

Spend a few minutes in prayer asking the Spirit to soften your heart. Pride and defensiveness will render this discussion useless. Pray for truth; it will win you over more quickly than another dose of "what you should do."

The word *rebuke* usually gives us a bad taste. It feels harsh, severe. And in modern English, that's pretty much true. But in Proverbs, when Solomon used the word *rebuke* in the original Hebrew, there were three distinct meanings:

1. *yakach* (used nine times): to prove, decide, reprove, be right, correct—and my favorite: to reason together
2. *ga'arah* (used three times): a reproof
3. *kalam* (used twice as the opposite of *discerning*. This behavior is forbidden in God's Word): to insult, shame, humiliate, blush, be put to confusion[8]

So as we are called to these first two definitions of rebuke, understand that it is never humiliating, judgmental, or shameful. It's not an angry pointing of the finger or a self-righteous indictment. That is not godly, nor does God approve that confrontation. Rather, it is a loving correction purely concerned with what is right. It is a moment between two believers when one tells the other, "This is not worthy of you. Can we reason it out together?"

Read the benefits of a loving rebuke in Proverbs 15:31; 17:10; 25:12. Write them out in your journal and consider one or more of the following questions.

- Proverbs 15:31
    - The wise believer *listens* to this correction. What inferior responses do we engage in besides listening?

- How is godly correction life giving? Have you ever been given back life in an area your friend was willing to confront?
- Proverbs 17:10
  - *Rebuke* here means "reproof," to prove again. God has already proven His truth in the Word, and sometimes our friend has to prove it again to us through an honest confrontation. Do you have an area where you are reluctant to believe God? Where you are stubborn toward a command? Resistant to a truth?
  - The New Life Version translates this verse like this: "A man of understanding learns more from being told the right thing to do than a fool learns from being beaten a hundred times." Do you learn from correction or repeat the same patterns? Why?
- Proverbs 25:12
  - Is this how you feel about receiving a rebuke? How would you describe it?
  - The wisdom of our girlfriends calls forth the beauty within us, even when our beauty is buried under sin. Has this ever happened to you? What beauty did your friend uncover for you?

Now read the consequences of rejecting a loving rebuke in Proverbs 1:29-31; 15:12. Work through the questions that the Spirit leads you to.

- Proverbs 1:29-31
  - What image do you get of this person? What is filling her heart? What is the bent of her personality?
  - Verse 31 in the New Living Translation says, "That is why they must eat the bitter fruit of living their

own way. They must experience the full terror of the path they have chosen." What would your life look like if you ran full tilt into a way you're choosing, particularly your trouble area?

- Have any of your friends been trying to warn you? How have you responded?

- Proverbs 15:12
  - Correction breeds resentment in those who won't listen to it. What happens to the girl who becomes overtaken by resentment? What does she eventually look like?
  - Do you consult your wise friends? Do you seek correction?
    - Bill Hybels suggests asking, "What would you like to say to me if you knew that I wouldn't get defensive and angry with you for telling me the truth?"[9]
    - Cloud and Townsend advise regularly asking these two questions: "What do I do that pushes you away from me? What do I do that draws you toward me?"[10]
      - How do you feel about asking these questions?

As a stubborn Type A girl, I'm in the trenches with you, Friends. Correction is hard to hear. It assaults our pride. Our first instinct is denial or justification, maybe some good old retaliation. At least those are my standbys.

But God is right. Just as our kids won't learn unless we teach them, show them, and discipline them, neither will we. And our girlfriends are often the compassionate messengers God uses. James suggests three strategies for hearing truth in 1:19:

1. Be quick to listen.
2. Be slow to speak.
3. Be slow to become angry.

When your insides are burning and your pride is mounting a counterattack, just stay quiet. That is not the time to have diarrhea of the mouth. Nod, make eye contact, listen. Tell your friend, "I know that was hard to say. Can you give me a little time to process this conversation and we'll take it further tomorrow?"

Dear Girls, the wise believer Solomon was talking about invites correction because she is interested in godliness. She is able to see past her defensiveness to her friend's loving concern. She accepts positive change as the avenue to wisdom.

But Solomon never said it didn't sting her. She didn't solicit random rebukes as an extracurricular activity. We don't see her declaring, "I *love* being corrected! It's fun and wonderful and it makes me feel *special!*" She wasn't immune to real emotions, nor do you have to be. You can tell your friend, "Ouch. This is stinging." You can even feel a little wounded.

But if you walk with the wise, the Holy Spirit can take your friend's brave confrontation and begin to work in you. He can replace your defensiveness with gratefulness. This is how He works. He uses the obedience of your girlfriend and the wisdom within you and produces a thing of beauty. He loves truth, and when you and your friend love it, too, together you form a divine conspiracy to be reckoned with.

Friendship Builders

Give Time

When we first moved to Austin, I got a random phone call from a girl named Molly. She needed friends who were home with small kids and were possibly on the verge of some sort of mental breakdown, so she called our pastor and asked if he had any suggestions. He offered my name. Big shock.

Molly and I started meeting about once a week so our kids could play, and we invited about four other moms to join us. Altogether, we had ten kids. Six years later, we have sixteen. We've been to every park, library, swimming pool, kids' event, snow cone stand, McDonald's, Chick-fil-A, museum, movie theater, and Barnes & Noble in Austin. Our husbands are all friends now. We've celebrated birthdays and holidays together. We've gone away for weekends together, sans kids, of course. Texas game day is a group event each season. Every one of our homes has been a gathering place: Molly cooks gourmet meals with sun-dried tomatoes and such; April bakes fat-free lasagna with whole wheat noodles and soy cheese; Stephanie makes homemade egg rolls; I order pizza, but we don't judge. I'm *very* good at other things.

We've prayed together, cried together, raised our kids together. Those girls are far more than fellow moms in the trenches. They're more than playmates. They are even more than friends. They have become sisters. Our lives have blended into something beautiful. And to accomplish that, we all pitched in. We gave something that was hard. It definitely required sacrifices. We could've spent it in a thousand other ways. But we decided our friendship was worth it.

We gave our time.

Girls, the best ideas for community aren't worth the paper they're printed on if we aren't willing to make time to execute them. There is no shortcut to intimacy. We can't expect the joys of community to just happen. There isn't a mystical formula for great friendships. Among healthy women, it is simply the result of time well spent together, then more time. And then a little more.

What is your gut reaction to making time for friendship? Do you have any concerns?

Karla Worley wrote,

Jesus indicated that this would be a measure of our success as His friends: time, attention, presence. To be there for my friend is to be Christlike, for Christ was literally "God with us," *Immanuel*. Jesus laid down His position, even His life, in order to be with us. I will have to lay down some of my benefits (leisure, rest, other relationships, personal goals) in order to be available for my friend. This is incarnation: Friend with me.[1]

🔊 Read about the first church in Acts 2:42-43. This was new. What do you see when you read this? What do you hear?

Listen, these Jews had lives, too. It's not like their jobs ceased to exist or their needs were miraculously diminished. Their kids still had school at the synagogue, and laundry had to be done. Women were still busy from the time their eyes opened to the moment they shut, before and after everyone else's, no doubt.

But hear it: *They devoted themselves.* That fellowship, that unity in Christ, was deemed worthy of their commitment. Girls, unity isn't fostered because we're nice people or have our acts together. It isn't some magical mystery. It is preserved because we work hard at it. Unity is realized when it is a priority. The end.

It's no different from anything else we consider important. If we want healthy bodies, we exercise and try to quit eating our kids' leftover fries. When we are pursuing professional success, we work diligently. If we need a vacation, we plan, save, organize, pack, drive. So if we want the bond of friendship, we put it squarely on our plate and say, "I'm doing this." We devote ourselves.

🔊 *Do you devote time to your girlfriends? If so, what do you do? If not, what has kept you from doing so?

Read Acts 2:44. List everything you can think of that you and your closest friends have in common.

Time together affords women immense relief because it allows us to become aware of the many things we have in common. "You can't get to school on time either? Your kids are fighting like Nazis, too? You're suffocating in guilt like I

am? Your husband also wants more sex than you're giving?"
Time spent together is like balm on our open wounds. We
enter into our dreams and struggles jointly; they're hardly
different. We learn from each other. There is nothing we are
completely alone in.

Outside of time together, we can't experience this camara-
derie. Women begin to feel isolated, shamed: *Surely no one feels
like I do. I'm the only one who struggles with this. Everyone else is
sailing through this issue.* On the contrary, I have never in my
life had a circumstance another friend hasn't experienced, too.
Not one. God brings us together, and there is marvelous unity
in our common ground.

It becomes holy ground.

Believer, trust me, you are not the only woman who has
experienced the following:

- Struggled with depression
- Lost her patience and yelled like a chimpanzee
- Had marital issues
- Had kids who behaved like derelicts
- Been mad, sad, or frustrated with God
- Had an unfulfilled dream
- Had a sordid history
- Suffered a terrible loss

It is during the time we offer each other that your story
and my story turn into our story. Your portion isn't all that
different from mine anyway. Yes, you are you, and I am me,
but we are both women, wives, maybe mothers, daughters of
God (feisty or otherwise), girls at heart. If you'll let me in, I'll
understand you. I promise.

*Read Acts 2:45. What is your experience with girl-friends who serve you and meet your needs? What have they done?

When my perfectly healthy daughter had her first seizure at age four, we went through three days of ER rooms, blood tests, MRIs, CT scans, spinal taps, EEGs, neurologists, raw fear. It's stunning how quickly life can turn around. I was exhausted. My daughter was spent. We didn't have answers yet, and we entered that awful period of waiting. Tears and terror left me broken.

On that third day, my Girlfriend Leslie offered me a gift. Of course, she'd been there in the ER; real friends come when you need them. They don't need to be asked. When the frenzy of the crisis was just behind us, she called and said, "Do you want to come over and just be normal? We can talk about hair products."

Precious friend.

Sometimes being there means saying, "I'll give you rest. I'll stand guard." We give each other a safe place to feel normal when we're anything but. And when we can't move forward, real friends take care of it. They'll clean your toilets and make your family dinner. They'll take your kids and take your calls. Sometimes they help us draw boundaries when we are unable to.

Girlfriends in Christ, if we are too busy to love each other like this, then we are too busy. At the end of the day, God placed the highest priority on relationships. Yes, our careers are fabulous and our schedules are purposeful, but they will not sit by a hospital bed with us or take the wheel on a road trip. And even our husbands and families cannot fill the space that a girlfriend can. We must love our friends and serve them with our time.

They'll do the same for us.

I'm not suggesting you make your friends your part-time job. Obviously our families and careers will require more of us. That's healthy, and it would be impractical to attempt equal balance here. But we must make *some* time to love our friends. They aren't the largest slice of the pie, but they are still a slice. Dear One, you can't wait for time to present itself for friend-ship. It will never do that. You must create it.

Who needs you right now? How can you serve her with your time?

Time is the breeding ground for memories, inside jokes, stories. It is where you and I progress from knowing about each other to knowing each other. It's how we make room for playing and laughing together. Time becomes service, offered through the loving hands of girlfriends. It is a string of moments in which we heal, grieve, grow. They are just minutes, but in them we find out we are not alone. You cannot put a value on that kind of discovery.

For some of you, time is the ultimate sacrifice—more than honesty, more than fear. It is the commodity you have the least of. So yet again, you are given the opportunity to take part in the ministry of your Savior. He did not offer the lesser sacri-fices, but He gave His very life. He prized friendship with you more highly than the breath in His lungs. He is Immanuel, God with us. With us at all costs.

Jesus' sacrifice gave us a relationship beyond value.

So will yours.

Ask God to evaluate your time. What portion of it is needed for your friends? Are you willing to give it? Pray for resolve. Time cannot be managed, only spent.

Give Grace

If time is the foundation for unity, then grace is the infrastructure that holds it up. The thing is that we are fragile people. At any moment, I could blow it. You could blurt something out. An attitude could surface that might send the whole mechanism reeling. New sins present themselves constantly. Fresh insecurities show their ugly faces every day. Just because I'm fine today doesn't mean I won't fall apart next month.

I sometimes think of the human race like a bunch of knees. Knees are so awkward and easily injured. Every other person has had surgery on one or both. I'd almost say God made an error, but I'm not in the mood to challenge His design today. They're made to bend forward, but they always want to bend backward, hyperextending themselves. Knees always have to be wrapped up, bandaged, iced down, soaked. Almost every knee is scarred. You occasionally meet a healthy knee, but one wrong step off the curb and it's going down, too.

So when a group of knees get together, they simply have to make room for grace. There is no way for them to function together if they establish a pecking order of previous injuries or those yet to happen. Because happen they will.

In general, how do you do at extending grace to other people? Is it conditional? Only to certain friends? Boundless?

"Grace wonderfully reorients all our relationships," wrote Thrall, McNicol, and Lynch in *TrueFaced*. "We no longer see one another with our sin between us. We no longer see one another through the grid of our shame, blame, and anger. . . . We no longer hide our real faces from each other. We begin to discover that our character is actually formed in relationships. We stand in front of each other, true-faced."[2]

*Read Colossians 3:11. What was Paul saying about our differences?

There are some nonnegotiables of godliness: love, patience, compassion. These are goals for every believer. But outside of the pillars, there are a thousand issues that are decided simply by our preferences. We have various styles and opinions; the bent of our personalities can take us in many different directions.

You may be passionate about homeschooling, whereas I am incapable of educating my own children and maintaining their status as "alive." I have a career (a loose term) and love it, but you may feel just as strongly about not working outside of your home. You believe in natural births; I asked for an epidural in my eighth month. I love this part of town, but you think that part is the place to live. Your philosophy is this; mine is that. Our house rules may differ. Our political affiliations run the gamut. I have these strong feelings that you might not share.

Do you see the need for grace?

*Are you sometimes threatened by the ways your close friends are different from you? Which ways bother you? Think critically.

Can you pinpoint why you feel that way?

Dear Girls, let your friend be herself. She doesn't have to be you. You may not agree with her, but give her grace in her preferences as long as they aren't hurting her. If she thinks this and you think that, it's okay! Let's widen the space we live in together. It is the immature heart that won't allow for diversity. It's probably not that you are so against her ideas, but her differing opinion feels like an indictment on your own. Maturity understands that her choices are not about you. Resist the urge to project them into your experience and celebrate them in her life instead.

My two women's ministry directors set a lovely example in this area. Teri is the bulldog, fast-paced, quick decision maker. She has a sharp wit and is in the what's-the-bottom-line camp. Elaine, on the other hand, is the gentle, soft-spoken, ultra slow decision maker. She is the tender heart and is in what I call the kind-and-precious camp. They are polar opposites, yet together they direct a giant ministry. They love the dichotomies in their relationship, and so they should.

Read Colossians 3:12. "Therefore" means in light of our inconsequential differences mentioned in verse 11, we are to behave as Paul instructs in verse 12. Of the five characteristics he gives, which do you struggle with most? Why is that?

So what does it really look like to clothe yourself in these qualities? It's a pretty sentence on paper, but how does it bear out? Girls, it isn't just in the big, preplanned moments that this kind of love is demonstrated. It's when your friend blows it and you choose kind words, rejecting disapproving body language. It happens when she makes a terrible decision and you wrap your arms around her neck and help her find grace. It shows up when your friend makes a choice opposite yours and you resist the urge to defend your stance or respond with sarcasm. It occurs when she does something you would never do and you clap out loud rather than launch into a dissertation on why *you* could never do that.

Grace is about what I can offer you, not what I can receive from you. I'm not asking you to replicate my decisions and become a chameleon to my personality. I can't expect you to bear the burden of my identity. That's too much pressure on you, and it's not your load to carry. When I lean on you for validation, grace is destroyed because I get disconnected from Christ, the Author of my worth.

A synonym for grace is *leniency*. I love that, because sometimes we are just too hard on each other. Our friend cannot be our Jesus. That's too hard for her. She is incapable of the perfection and omnipotence that role requires. She can't chart your course or heal your wounds. She is unaware of the number of hairs on your head, even if she knows who styles them. Give her the grace she needs to do what she does best: be your friend, be herself.

Read Colossians 3:13. Here we go. Why is this the hardest offering of grace?

In the original Greek, *bear with* literally meant "to hold up."[3] When our friend hurts us, our instinct is to push her down, push her away. But Girls, if she was ugly, if she chose gossip, if she betrayed you, Satan knocked her legs squarely out from under her. He tempted her with selfishness, baited her with justification. He whispered, "It's okay. She won't know.

She won't care. This is about you. There is no real harm here." Then when the fallout came, she was left alone, slammed with shame and regret.

So if we are to forgive as Jesus did us, then we pick our friend up off the floor of her bad choices, wrap an arm around her waist, and hold her up. We recognize that although it was ultimately her doing, she was also a target, and destroying unity was the bull's-eye. And by the way, Satan is counting on your anger to up the ante. Holding each other up on the heels of hurt feelings is the ultimate extension of grace. This is when we lean into Jesus and pray for that mind of His that Paul said we have (1 Corinthians 2:16).

*Have you chosen to push someone away rather than hold her up after she hurt you? How is that working out?

Again, I'm not asking you to be foolish. Some people will hurt you habitually with no remorse or attempts to make amends. To continue making yourself available to them is unwise. But when your safe friends hurt you, then it's time for this level of Jesus forgiveness. Cloud and Townsend predict, "One of the greatest benefits you'll find in your safe settings is a deepening understanding of failure and what to do with it."[4] It is a relief to discover that your friend can fail you, you can forgive her, and no one will die. There is much life after forgiveness.

*Finally, read Colossians 3:14-15. How do we let the peace of Christ rule in our hearts?

Yes, we are a bunch of knees. I've got one good one, one bad one. You've got scars. Maybe yours pop like firecrackers when you get out of bed. Mine do. It's weird. But the love of Jesus is the tie that binds us together. He gently wraps up our tired knees, preparing them for use. He covers up the injuries we inflict on each other, enabling us to go the distance together. The love He has for you and me is enough. If I let Jesus fill me up and you do the same, He'll lead us to that perfect unity we're looking for. And there is nothing more beautiful than grace between two girlfriends.

Put on love.

Be thankful.

Will you fill your friendships with grace? Ask the Spirit to endow you with mercy, leniency, forgiveness. He can do it, even if you are unable to.

Serve Together

God understands my ADD factor, so He usually gives me one project at a time. My propensity for melodrama and distraction is staggering. So when I landed a five-book contract—this study being the final project—He administered immediate damage control on the front end to keep me from spazzing out. Graciously, He pulled me out of a key role in our church women's ministry and tucked me back into a cozy corner for the next three years so I could write in some sort of focused manner.

That cozy corner was the Thursday night Bible study I reference constantly. Talk about laid back. The biggest detail was making sure we had a sweet *and* a salty snack every week, and I passed that off to middle management. Those girls have transformed into the dearest, most beloved friends. They've seen me through every book, each fresh insecurity, ministry travels, struggles. We've worked through infertility, marriage heartaches, death, sex (to be a fly on *that* wall), motherhood, history. We've welcomed new husbands and new babies. We've journeyed through eight books of the Bible, laboring over every detail. Together, we've truly discovered the unity of Christ.

So when God began revealing to me several months ago that my time in the cozy corner was almost up, I started grieving. The sacrifices of ministry sometimes overwhelm me, and I got mad. "No. I won't go. I need this, God! Don't you care about me? Don't you know how much I love them?"

And God said, "Yes. I care. I know. You and your friends are going to minister *together*." And as one precious season closed, we entered a new one. We are now offering all we've learned about God and community to our church. Together, we're launching a new study on a big scale. We're out of the living room and into the sanctuary. I'm teaching; my girlfriends are small-group leaders. They are running registration and sending e-mails. They're putting together materials and planning. They are greeting at the door and setting up chairs. God tucked us away to pour into us and then pulled us forward to share the love.

The only thing better than serving God is serving Him with girlfriends. For function, for fellowship, two is better than one. It always has been. The Bible is very encouraging in this area, Girls. Let's see today how God truly commissions us together.

Two years into Jesus' three-year ministry, the time came to empower His disciples to carry on His mission. They considered themselves students, not yet ready to graduate from Jesus' School of Hard Knocks. But He had only one year left, a year wrought with opposition. So ready or not, off He sent them.

📽️ Read Mark 6:7. How do you guess working in pairs helped the disciples?

How do you think it helped the ministry?

"We keep forgetting that we are being sent out two by two," wrote Henri Nouwen. "We cannot bring good news on our own. We are called to proclaim the Gospel together, in community. You might have already discovered how radically different traveling alone is from traveling together. I have found over and over again how hard it is to be truly faithful to Jesus when I am alone."[5]

That's an honest assessment, one that Jesus fully understood. The dangers are vast: Alone, our weariness can overtake us. We start questioning the task we're on: *Did God really want me to do this?* Opposition stings worse when we are the sole recipient. Decisions can get overwhelming when no one else speaks wisdom into them. We become sitting ducks for distraction, temptation, frustration, pride. The messenger can become more valued than the message, a risk in our hero-worship culture.

Have you ever experienced any of this damage by serving alone? What happened?

Read Mark 6:8-11. Where do you see community in this passage?

Jesus was a really smart guy. I generally trust what He said in Scripture, especially if trust can be defined as acting sort of grabby and neurotic. So He concluded that the pairs didn't need to bring food or water, a suitcase or money. No extra clothes, no travel arrangements. No typical securities or comforts. No guarantees, no safeguards. No just-in-case items or basic necessities.

He told them to bring two things:

A staff.

And a friend.

Girls, we need each other if we are to serve as Jesus called us to. This is a baseline necessity in ministry. I get distracted sometimes with the details: The online registration is messing up, the book table is lame, the materials aren't packaged cutely enough. How is my message? How is my presentation? How is my hair?

But Jesus asks, "Who is with you?" Believer, in your area of service, who is with you? What are you good at, and who can go there with you? What can you and your girlfriends accomplish together? We read in Ecclesiastes,

> Two are better than one,
> > because they have a good return for their
> > work. (4:9)

What I can achieve alone cannot compare to what we can do together.

Do you know your spiritual gifts? What are they? If you're not sure, what are you good at? What do you love? What do you have to offer?

*How could you partner with a friend (or friends) to serve God in this area?

Not only is this infinitely more effective, but it's also a blast. It brings two favorites together. Doing what God created us for satisfies the deepest parts of us, but doing it with girlfriends is having your cake, eating it, too, and discovering that cooking butter makes it fat free. It deepens your love for each other while accomplishing God's work. Everyone wins.

Anne Lamott says that no one gets into heaven without a letter of reference from the poor. That's more or less what Jesus said, too. So my girlfriends Carson, Christi, Laura, Laurie, and I adopted a family in Austin who were evacuees of Hurricane Katrina. Our new friend Leslie has seven kids, two jobs, no husband, and a lot of responsibility. Together, we've come under her, provided for Christmas, assisted her job search, attended financial counseling with her, handled school supplies, brought groceries. We've tried to serve her with pure hearts and selfless motives.

Not only are we able to care for a worthy family, but I've also seen a side of my girlfriends that I hadn't seen before. I am humbled by their compassion and work ethic. I've learned how to cast off judgment for mercy. They've shown me how. I've held hands with them and prayed for this family we adore. When I see them hug Leslie's neck or haggle with a bill collector on her behalf, I love them more. I see what Jesus was getting at.

*Have you ever served with your friend? How did it affect your relationship?

This is more than a good idea. It's how we should approach service. It's how we should approach friendship. As my friend in Christ, you are more than my Girls' Night Out partner; you are my partner in ministry. God repeatedly stamped this strategy with His approval:

> After this the Lord appointed seventy-two others and sent them *two by two* ahead of him to every town and place where he was about to go. (Luke 10:1)

> The Holy Spirit said, "Set apart for me *Barnabas and Saul* for the work to which I have called them." . . . The two of them, sent on their way by the Holy Spirit, went down to Seleucia and sailed from there to Cyprus. (Acts 13:2,4)

We are sending *Judas and Silas* to confirm by word of mouth what we are writing. (Acts 15:27)

He sent two of his helpers, *Timothy and Erastus*, to Macedonia, while he stayed in the province of Asia a little longer. (Acts 19:22)

Greet *Priscilla and Aquila*, my fellow workers in Christ Jesus. They risked their lives for me. (Romans 16:3-4)

Greet also the church that meets at their house. (Romans 16:5)

Dear One, if you want the laugh-out-loud joys of friendship, serve together. Take your relationship to the next level. Make a space for God's work right in the middle of your friendship. No one will love serving with you more than your girlfriend. She'll laugh with you, maybe at you, as you push through ministry together. She won't expect you to be perfect or extraspiritual. In fact, if you acted like you were, she'd call your bluff. Just as it is a wonderful surprise to watch your husband turn into a daddy, it's incredible to see your girlfriend become your cominister in the kingdom.

Imagine what you can accomplish together.

He told them, "The harvest is plentiful, but the workers are few. Ask the Lord of the harvest, therefore, to send out workers into his harvest field. Go! I am sending you out like lambs among wolves." (Luke 10:2-3)

Ask the Spirit how He'd like to use you and your friends. If you are already serving together, ask if there is anyone else you can invite into your mission.

Laugh Together

Some moments can be enjoyed correctly only with girlfriends. Our husbands try their best, but as the wise old proverb says, girls just wanna have fun. So when my thirtieth birthday reared its head, my ten closest girlfriends stepped in to take matters into their entertaining hands.

They took me to a favorite restaurant on South Congress, and we enjoyed dinner like a bunch of married girls do: sharing entrees, passing bites around, ordering the cream sauce on the side and then dumping it all on anyway, flirting with the waitstaff. From there, they'd booked rooms in an urban bed-and-breakfast with a view of the Austin skyline. As we walked the grounds, they led me to an upstairs deck they'd strung with lights, thirty lit candles, and comfy chairs. By the chair of honor were thirty presents for thirty years.

Every present was about me and my favorite things: sour candy, magazine subscriptions, hair products, big earrings, favorite movies, fresh flowers. Each friend also gave me a verse; some regifted verses I'd given them at one point, while others gave verses that described our friendship in Christ. They wrote out memories and inside jokes. We laughed until we were sick.

We cried until we started laughing again.

In the spirit of the slumber party, we had a pillow fight that got us in trouble with the neighbors. We slept three to a bed, giggling and talking for hours. We shared a leisurely breakfast the next morning and spent the rest of the day shopping in downtown boutiques that we never frequent because all of us shop at Target and Old Navy.

I am the luckiest friend in the world (or blessed, if you believe in that sort of thing).

If time is the foundation for unity and grace is the infrastructure that holds it up, then laughter is the air-conditioning, plush carpeting, cushiony armchairs, and stocked pantry. Friendship among women whispers of the delights of heaven. What is more precious than hearing women laugh until no sound comes out? Of seeing them enjoy each other? Oh, Girls, we are so favored to be women!

What friends do you enjoy being around most? What is the tone of your relationship?

Read Ecclesiastes 9:3-6. (Solomon got cranky in his later years.) How would you paraphrase this passage in one or two sentences?

I don't want to focus on dead lions here. And I'm not intending to set a negative tone on our last structured day together, so this will be brief. But I want you to hear this: You have one shot at this life, Precious Girl. One. You'll never get a day back that you wasted on loneliness, pessimism, or regret. Any hate that you guarded won't have produced the justice you waited for. That jealousy you wore won't have leveled the playing field like you were hoping it would. A life wasted in bitterness is a life wasted, Dear Friend. A whole life lost.

Anyone who is among the living has hope. There is still

time to run into the arms of laughter, love, friendship that smacks of God. There is still time to speak blessings into the lives of your friends and receive love with open arms. There is time to create memories and get side pains from laughing with your girlfriends. While there is breath in your lungs, you have hope. Don't waste that breath another day.

It's not too late.

Read Ecclesiastes 9:7-8. What was Solomon getting at? Summarize his thoughts.

*How easy is it for you to do what he describes? Why is that?

We are dressed in white, Believers, the color of the redeemed. God said of our eternity, "They will walk with me, dressed in white, for they are worthy" (Revelation 3:4). The girl who knows she is worthy is free to laugh. She's free to love without bounds. She welcomes in gladness and enjoys life. She is fully present. Girls, we must show up every day and live that day well. Today is the only day we'll have just like it.

The Message paraphrases this passage,

Seize life! Eat bread with gusto,
    Drink wine with a robust heart.
    Oh yes—God takes pleasure in *your* pleasure!

And what better pleasure to experience than in each other? Laugh. Giggle with your friends. Be silly. Be funny. Exchange complaining for complimenting. Do something crazy. Wear hats on Girls' Night Out. Run a 5K together. Laugh at each other for being out of shape. Go to funny movies. Tell funny stories. Eat food together with gladness. Drink wine together with joyful hearts.

God's favor shines down on this.

Do you need to stop wishing and start living? What will you do first? Who will you call? What ideas will you come up with? Make a plan.

Girls, enjoying life together means someone has to pull the trigger. My Girlfriend April mentioned at church recently how she was missing everyone. Didn't we deserve a girls' night? I begged her to send an e-mail to our friends, she did it that day, we put a date on the calendar, and we all showed up. Simple as that. We shut the restaurant down and laughed so hard that I came home with facial fatigue.

Neglect is easy; anyone can do it. It's how friends lose a month, a year, ten years. The friends who stick are those who say, "I'm committed to laughing with and at you for as long as we're both able." We put on gladness and joy and wrap it in diligence.

You know what else we do? We go away together. There is nothing like a road trip with girlfriends. Does that sound crazy to you? Girls do it all the time, and they're no different from you. Their lives are busy, too. Their husbands also panic at the idea of taking care of the kids for three days. Their trips require sacrificing, saving, planning, and sweet talking, just like yours would. It is not the nonbusy women who make this a priority; it's the busy women who make it happen despite their busyness.

There are a million options: Have a slumber party at a girl-friend's house (of *course* we're not too old), go to a bed-and-breakfast, drive to a conference together, check in for a night at a swanky hotel, take a real trip and use someone's birthday as an excuse, go camping, take a shopping trip to the nearest big city, go to a theme park, rent a cabin, create an adventure, meet in a city you've always wanted to see.

*What are your concerns with this? Are you scared to ask your hubby? Worried about time? Money? Kids?

*How can you address those concerns?

Honestly, would life fall apart while you took an adventure with your girlfriends? One night even? Can your husband dial the phone? Then he can order pizza and keep the wheels on while you're gone. Need a place for your kids? Ask mom. Trade with a friend. Hire a babysitter. Use your sister. Exchange a favor. No money? Don't spend any. Have a slumber party and bring the salsa that's in your fridge. No time? If you plan a trip three months from now, you'll make the time, same as anything else.

I don't want to breathe my last breath filled with regret. I don't want to say, "I wish I had. . . ." I want a life full of memories and albums full of pictures. I want my old, wrinkled, gray-headed girlfriends to sit on the porch with me and laugh about our adventures. I want to show my grandchildren pictures of me and my friends standing in Times Square, arms linked. I want to run this race for the prize of unity, laughter, and a fully lived life.

I want to love well.
I want to let others love me well, too.
I want to laugh.
I want to be glad.
I want to enjoy the women in my life.
I want to embrace the unity of Christ.
I want my girlfriends around until my last day.

Don't you?

From now on, will you commit to enjoying your girl-friends? Ask the Spirit to fill you with laughter. Pray for hope; it's never too late for the living.

DAY FIVE

Dig In: Speaking Blessings

So here we are, Girlfriends in Christ. I trust God for the prayers I've offered on your behalf. I believe Him for the work He has done and will do as you walk toward unity. This is a narrow road we're walking, one traveled by very few. We simply cannot bear to travel it alone; it's already a tough journey. But together, we find strength, we hold one another up, we carry our friend when she can't walk on her own. Sometimes we skip downhill; other times we pull each other up the incline. God hedges us in through His Word, His Spirit. We are safe, even when we're weary.

We'll close this week by exploring a gift we have to offer to our friends. In Latin, the word *bless* is *benedicere*. The word *benediction* used in many churches literally means speaking (diction) well (bene). Girls, we have the power to speak blessings into the lives of our friends. We can speak well of them, to them, about them to Christ.

"According to Hebrew thought patterns," wrote Karla Worley, "the spoken word had a life of its own. It was not just an idea; it was a happening. When Isaac gave Jacob his blessing, rather than Esau, it was an act, a thing which had been done and could not be taken back. As well, the word, once spoken, had the power to fulfill itself. It could cause itself *to be*. To speak a blessing on someone was to cause them to be blessed."[6]

Spend a few minutes in prayer asking the Holy Spirit to prepare your heart for His Word. Ask Him to open your eyes and receive His leadership today.

Psalm 115 was basically a blessing the priests spoke over people at the temple. As they gathered together in God's name, God's servants empowered the nation through a word spoken well.

Read Psalm 115:1-8.

- Why do you think the blessing began like this? What were the priests establishing?
- Giving blessings does not mean turning your friends into idols, even if you admire them. How might flattery contradict a blessing?
- We don't seek to glorify each other. That's God's place of honor. What blessing can you speak to God? How is He magnificent to you?

Read Psalm 115:9-11.

- Has anyone ever spoken blessings like this to you? How did it affect your life?
- We hold the words of life. Do you need to urge a friend to trust God right now? Who? Can you help point out how He is her help? Her shield?
- Is there a household you need to speak well to? About? On their behalf? What can you say to cause them to be blessed?

- Do you have a blessing you're withholding? Why are you reluctant to say it?

Read Psalm 115:12-15.

- Blessings are the greatest affirmations we can offer. How can you affirm a friend's position in God? Does someone need to hear you say, "You belong to Him"?
- Do you have a friend who feels small? How can you reorient her within the blessings God has reserved for her? Can you call forth her fear of God?
- Girls, do you need to speak the blessings of fruitfulness to a girlfriend? Will you speak well to God on her behalf, asking for increase?
- Do you have a friend who is on the cusp of a dream? A task? A new place? A calling? Who is it? Would you be willing to pray over her, "May you be blessed by the LORD, the Maker of heaven and earth"?

Read Psalm 115:16-18.

- Together, you and your friend can worship. What does that look like as you journey on as friends?
- How do we adjust so that we can praise God with our friends for the rest of our days? How do we keep those priorities active?
- Do you have a friend who needs to hear that she is a part of God's whole family? That she stands in worship among God's nations? How can you speak well to her?

Henri Nouwen wrote, "[A blessing] is more than a word of praise or appreciation; it is more than pointing out someone's talents or good deeds; it is more than putting someone in the light. To give a blessing is to affirm, to say 'yes' to a person's Belovedness."[7]

Your friends are beloved in so many ways. They are beautiful in spirit, adored by the Father. Who they are is wonderful—well beyond what they do. They are joint heirs with Jesus. Take that one to the bank. They are mothers who sacrifice without blinking, wives who love their husbands in immeasurable ways. They are redeemed, dressed in white, and worthy. They bring joy and laughter to the lucky ones who know them.

We have the privilege to speak this truth into their lives, to call it forth. We can speak well every single day to our girlfriends:

"Your heart is true and good. Your motives are pure."
"God will never leave you. You are His favorite."
"Thank you for carrying the load for me."
"Let me show you this verse. It's for you."
"God has set you apart. You are worthy of this task."
"You make me stronger."
"I love you."

Jesus said, "The words I have spoken to you are spirit and they are life" (John 6:63). Aren't they? Jesus has spoken life into millions of hearts. And we are called to imitate our Savior. We have life-giving power in the blessings we speak. When you tell me I am able in Christ, I am. When I tell you that your heart is beautiful, it becomes more so. When we tell each other that our friendship is valuable, it grows.

So, Dear Ones, throw open the doors to your heart and love your friends well. Let love in. I hope you've discovered the joys of traveling together. It's not easy. It's not always comfortable. It requires some tough moments. It's not for the fainthearted. But it speaks of the unity between Jesus and His Father. And that, my Friends, is worth the journey. In the spirit of Paul, who has taught us so well, let me close by saying:

Greet your girlfriends in Christ—a friend of yours is a friend of mine. Greet the church that loves and supports you. My girlfriends send their greetings; they've prayed for you relentlessly, though they don't know your faces. Greet one another with a holy kiss.

Finally, Girlfriends, be of one mind. Live in love and peace. Embrace truth. Lavish one another with grace. I pray the God of grace will fill you utterly and unite you completely. And may the fellowship of the Spirit keep you all. I hope to see you face to face. I love you.

Leader's Guide

For this study, each woman will need:

1. A copy of *Girl Talk*
2. A Bible (most references included come from the NIV)
3. A lined journal

Girl Talk is a five-week study. Each week requires five days of homework, about thirty to forty minutes each day. I suggest that leaders stay at least a week ahead in the study in order to offer advance guidance if necessary. The ideal size for a small group is eight to twelve women.

In my church, the whole women's ministry gathers as a large group each week (for worship and a brief teaching session) and then women divide into small groups to discuss the study. In other words, all the small groups meet in the same building at the same time. In this case, I've found it helpful to have a leaders' meeting each week just before the large session. Fifteen minutes together in prayer and discussion have provided an opportunity to address many issues before they came up in small groups. Leaders can discuss complicated questions and anticipate weekly challenges in advance.

If the small groups meet in separate places, such as homes, perhaps you can have a weekly online dialogue or can pair up leaders so they have a partner to encourage them. Supported leaders are happier leaders.

The small-group discussion should take sixty to ninety minutes, depending on the size and personality of the group. Feel free to supplement that time with worship, activities, or a large-group session.

Each week, set the example by having your Bible and book open and ready. Begin each session with prayer, asking God to inhabit your conversation and increase your faith.

Have your girls open their books to Days 1–4. The questions marked with an asterisk (*) are good discussion questions to pose. There are two to four marked in each day of study. Look ahead at the designated questions to prepare adequately for discussion. Most of the questions selected involve personal application of the study, but by all means keep bringing in the Scripture that sets them up. And if your group obviously wants to pursue a different point, don't squash the Spirit's leading.

Create an atmosphere of authenticity by voicing your own thoughts and struggles. Keep conversation moving and work hard to include all four days in discussion. If you aim to spend roughly fifteen minutes on each day's questions, Days 1–4 will take about an hour to cover.

When Days 1–4 have been discussed, refer to Day 5. As this is a personal prayer and journaling activity, wrap up your conversation by asking, "What was the biggest thing you took away from this day? This week? What did the Spirit teach you in prayer and journaling?"

Close each weekly session in prayer. Make an effort to change your prayer techniques each week.

- Try partner praying—two girls share immediate needs and pray over each other.
- You could lead the group in sentence prayer—only *one* or *two* sentences voiced at a time ("Help me let my guard down." "Thank you for the women in my life."). Explain this technique first and model it by beginning with a one-sentence prayer. When you think the girls are done, close in a brief final prayer.
- You could lead them through silent prayer using prompts from Scripture. For example, open to Psalm 66. Read verses 1-4 aloud and say, "Praise God for His awesome deeds in your life. Who has He been for you?" Give group members two or three minutes to pray silently; then read verses 5-7 and say, "How has God delivered you? What has He done on your behalf?" Allow them to pray silently, and continue through Scripture prompts as you see fit. This can be done with any passage you are drawn to or one that seems to uniquely fit your group.
- You could pray Scripture. Choose a passage such as Psalm 33 or Exodus 15:1-18. Have each woman open her Bible to the chosen passage. Tell the group that you will read the whole passage aloud and then they will choose a line or phrase they'd like to pray again to God ("In your unfailing love you will lead the people you have redeemed"). Allow them to speak various verses randomly as God leads them. They might speak several times each over the course of the prayer. When it seems they are done, close briefly with a final prayer.
- Try word prompts. For example, go through the following list, saying each prompt out loud and

allowing the women to complete the sentence with one or two words:

- "God, You are . . ."
- "You've given me . . ."
- "Your words are . . ."
- "Help me to . . ."
- "Show me how to . . ."
- "Thank You for . . ."
- "I heard You tell me . . ."

After each prompt, allow the women to respond until you think they're done and then move on to the next prompt. Choose sentence starters appropriate to the week of study. Close with a brief prayer when finished.

- If your group is small enough, you could try intercessory prayer. Take turns praying over each group member individually. For example, put Jen in the middle. Each woman in turn prays two or three sentences over her. Think brief. Then move to Sarah and pray over her individually. It is a special way for your small group to connect with God in sweet intercession.
- Brainstorm with the other leaders on various prayer techniques. This is a wonderful place to teach creative prayer by example. Anything goes as long as God's name is honored.

Consider a celebration, dinner, party, day trip, anything fun at the close of the study. *Girl Talk* is a celebration of togetherness. Your girls will have shared, cried, learned from each other. God called us His family. You know He loves to see the kids getting along. Small groups should foster fellowship as much as learning.

I love group cohesion, and I'm a big fan of longevity with the same girls. My small group met together for three years, and it got better and better. Where we are now versus where we began cannot even be compared. We began as students of the Word (mostly strangers), and now we're sisters.

Karla Worley put it like this in *Traveling Together*:

How can you, my friend in the faith, help me to become more like Christ? You can know me. You can be there. Hold me accountable for holy living. Encourage me to live the life of the Spirit. Model servanthood. Keep me active in worship and service. And you can do all this in the course of our days and years together, not just doing holy things, but understanding that all the things we do hold the possibility of the holy.[1]

Leaders, nurture friendships. Create authenticity. Make opportunities for real connection available. The longer you laugh and cry and pray together, the stronger this journey gets.

Notes

WEEK ONE: TOGETHER

1. John and Stasi Eldredge, *Captivating* (Nashville: Nelson, 2005), 27.
2. Henri J. M. Nouwen, *My Sister, My Brother* (Ijamsville, MD: Word Among Us Press, 2005), 15.
3. Harry Stack Sullivan, quoted in John Powell, *Why Am I Afraid to Tell You Who I Am?* (Allen, TX: Resources for Christian Living, 1998), 39.
4. Noam Chomsky, *The Prosperous Few and the Restless Many* (Tuscon, AZ: Odonian Press, 1993), excerpt found at http://www.thirdworldtraveler.com/Chomsky/ChomOdon_Divide.html.
5. Larry Crabb, *Connecting* (Nashville: W Publishing, 1997), 89.
6. www.biblegateway.com/quicksearch/?quicksearch=children
7. Dee Brestin, *We Are Sisters* (Colorado Springs, CO: Life Journey, 2006), 39.
8. Dr. Henry Cloud and Dr. John Townsend, *Boundaries* (Grand Rapids, MI: Zondervan, 1992), 75.
9. Dr. Henry Cloud and Dr. John Townsend, *Safe People* (Grand Rapids, MI: Zondervan, 1995), 68.

Week Two: Truth or Dare

1. *Random House Unabridged Dictionary*, s.v. "truth," 2006, http://dictionary.reference.com/browse/truth.
2. Dr. Henry Cloud and Dr. John Townsend, *Safe People* (Grand Rapids, MI: Zondervan, 1995), 74.
3. Cloud and Townsend, *Safe People*, 75.
4. John Powell, *Why Am I Afraid to Tell You Who I Am?* (Allen, TX: Resources for Christian Living, 1998), 98.
5. Cloud and Townsend, *Safe People*, 66.
6. Henri J. M. Nouwen, *My Sister, My Brother* (Ijamsville, MD: Word Among Us Press, 2005), 17.
7. Bill Hybels, Kevin Harney, and Sherry Harney, *The Real Deal* (Grand Rapids, MI: Zondervan, 1997), 19–20, 22.
8. www.bible.crosswalk.com/commentaries/MatthewHenryComplete/mhc-com.
9. "The Tax Collectors: History," *Bible History Online*, 2002, http://www.bible-history.com/taxcollectors/TAXCOLLECTORSHistory.htm.
10. Bill Thrall, Bruce McNicol, and John Lynch, *TrueFaced* (Colorado Springs, CO: NavPress, 2004), 16.

Week Three: Where Have All the Good People Gone?

1. Dr. Henry Cloud and Dr. John Townsend, *Safe People* (Grand Rapids, MI: Zondervan, 1995), 21.
2. Bill Thrall, Bruce McNicol, and John Lynch, *TrueFaced* (Colorado Springs, CO: NavPress, 2004), 43.
3. Cloud and Townsend, *Safe People*, 143–144.
4. Karla Worley, *Traveling Together* (Birmingham, AL: New Hope Publishers, 2003), 201.
5. Much thanks to Dr. Henry Cloud and Dr. John Townsend this week for their godly insight on developing healthy relationships, as thoroughly offered in their book *Safe People*. See 111–122.

6. Cloud and Townsend, *Safe People*, 113.

7. John Powell, *Why Am I Afraid to Tell You Who I Am?* (Allen, TX: Resources for Christian Living, 1998), 47.

8. Cloud and Townsend, *Safe People*, 122.

9. John MacArthur, *The MacArthur Bible Handbook* (Nashville: Nelson, 2003), 496.

Week Four: The Gift of Gab

1. Ellen Goodman and Patricia O'Brien, *I Know Just What You Mean* (New York: Simon & Schuster, 2000), 34–35.

2. John Powell, *Why Am I Afraid to Tell You Who I Am?* (Allen, TX: Resources for Christian Living, 1998), 47–54.

3. Karla Worley, *Traveling Together* (Birmingham, AL: New Hope Publishers, 2003), 55.

4. Bill Hybels, Kevin Harney, and Sherry Harney, *The Real Deal* (Grand Rapids, MI: Zondervan, 1997), 10.

5. Powell, 55.

6. Hybels, Harney, and Harney, 35–39.

7. Henri J. M. Nouwen, *My Sister, My Brother* (Ijamsville, MD: Word Among Us Press, 2005), 98.

8. "The Old Testament Hebrew Lexicon," crosswalk.com, http://bible.crosswalk.com/Lexicons/OldTestamentHebrew/heb.cgi?search=rebuke&version=nas&type=eng&submit=Find.

9. Hybels, Harney, and Harney, 57.

10. Dr. Henry Cloud and Dr. John Townsend, *Safe People* (Grand Rapids, MI: Zondervan, 1995), 180.

Week Five: Friendship Builders

1. Karla Worley, *Traveling Together* (Birmingham, AL: New Hope Publishers, 2003), 81.

2. Bill Thrall, Bruce McNicol, and John Lynch, *TrueFaced* (Colorado Springs, CO: NavPress, 2004), 71.

3. "The KJV New Testament Greek Lexicon," crosswalk.com, http://bible.crosswalk.com/Lexicons/Greek/grk.cgi?number =430&version=kjv.

4. Dr. Henry Cloud and Dr. John Townsend, *Safe People* (Grand Rapids, MI: Zondervan, 1995), 182.

5. Henri J. M. Nouwen, *My Sister, My Brother* (Ijamsville, MD: Word Among Us Press, 2005), 90.

6. Worley, 151.

7. Nouwen, 99.

Leader's Guide

9. Karla Worley, *Traveling Together* (Birmingham, AL: New Hope Publishers, 2003), 43.

About the Author

Jen Hatmaker has served alongside her husband, Brandon, in full-time ministry for twelve years. Six of those years have been at their current post, Lake Hills Church in Austin, where amazingly no one has asked them to leave. While serving women through teaching and writing, Jen has taken it upon herself to discover whether it's possible to love Jesus whole-heartedly and still have a teeny addiction to reality TV. She and Jesus are still working that one out.

Jen is the mother of three "lively" children, which is a euphemism for loud. Some people say they come by that honestly (from their dad's side, obviously). Gavin (eight), Sydney (six), and Caleb (four) are clearly unimpressed with Jen's speaking and writing; when Sydney peered into Jen's first box of books ever released, she glanced up and asked indifferently, "What's for dinner?"

Jen's girlfriends continue to be collaborators on her various ministry pursuits, such as making sure that right before an event she doesn't get a drastic haircut she's incapable of styling, and covering for her when she spends too much money on a pair of boots ("She needs to look impeccable in front of a crowd, Brandon."). They are very spiritually mature in these areas, and should you need to borrow them, their phone numbers are listed on Jen's website.

By a sheer act of God, Jen has written four other books, including *A Modern Girl's Guide to Bible Study: A Refreshingly Unique Look at God's Word*, *Road Trip: Five Adventures You're Meant to Live*, *Tune In: Hearing God's Voice Through the Static*, and *Make Over: Revitalizing the Many Roles You Fill*, all with NavPress.

Jen would love to speak at your event! To find out more information about her ministry or to contact her, visit her online at www.jenhatmaker.com.

MORE FUN AND ENTERTAINING BOOKS FROM JEN HATMAKER!

Make Over

ISBN-13: 978-1-57683-894-5
ISBN-10: 1-57683-894-3

Jen Hatmaker believes that there's a need for a new kind of Bible study to help women balance the many roles they play. *Make Over* delivers rich, relevant biblical content in a fun, casual voice. It features thirty-minute devotionals in a simple six-week format that fits into any schedule.

Road Trip

ISBN-13: 978-1-57683-892-1
ISBN-10: 1-57683-892-7

Road trips are as much about the journey as they are their ultimate destinations, and who better to travel with than your best Girlfriends? You navigate life together, why not the Bible? Guided by Abram, the Samaritan woman, Peter, Paul, and Jesus Himself, you're guaranteed the trip of a lifetime!

Tune In

ISBN-13: 978-1-57683-893-8
ISBN-10: 1-57683-893-5

God has given us the tools and written them down for us to read and study, but have we learned how to really tune in to them? You may think you've got a one-sided relationship with God, but He's in constant dialogue with you. Are you ready to tune Him in?

To order copies, visit your local Christian bookstore, call NavPress at 1-800-366-7788, or log on to www.navpress.com.
To locate a Christian bookstore near you, call 1-800-991-7747.

NAVPRESS
BRINGING TRUTH TO LIFE
www.navpress.com